How to Craft Killer Dialogue

for Fiction & Creative Non-Fiction

by Andrea J. Johnson

Guidebooks for Success

WRITER PRODUCTIVITY SERIES - BOOK 3

How to Craft Killer Dialogue. Copyright © 2023 by Andrea J. Johnson. Manufactured in the United States of America. All rights reserved. No part of this work may be sampled, copied, reproduced, distributed, stored in a database or information repository for later use, nor transmitted in any form or by any means (electronic, mechanical, or otherwise invented) without prior written consent by the author. Any replication of the text without the author's permission, except brief quotations in the context of a book review, is a violation of the copyright. First edition.

This book is for personal use only. Readers are responsible for undertaking any due diligence regarding the validity of the techniques and advice contained herein, and the author is not liable for any loss or damage caused by this book's use.

ISBN: 978-1-7376880-4-4 (ebook)

ISBN: 978-1-7376880-5-1 (paperback)

1. Fiction—Technique. 2. Authorship. 3. Dialogue. I. Title.

To receive a monthly email newsletter full of free writing advice and updates about future Writer Productivity Series books, register at https://ajthenovelist.com/sign-up/

About the Author

Andrea J. Johnson is an author and book coach who has written for the women's lifestyle brands *Popsugar* and *The List Daily*. She has also developed several craft articles for websites such as *CrimeReads*, *LitReactor*, *Funds for Writers*, and *DIY MFA*. She holds a B.A. in English from Swarthmore College, a copyediting certification from UC San Diego, and an M.F.A. in Writing Popular Fiction from Seton Hill University. In addition, she teaches Creative Writing and African American literature at the University of Maryland Eastern Shore. But most notably, she is the author of the Victoria Justice Mysteries about a trial stenographer turned amateur sleuth (think *Murder, She Wrote* meets the *The Pelican Brief*) and the mastermind behind the sensational genre guides *Mastering the Art of Suspense*, *How to Craft a Killer Cozy Mystery*, and *How to Craft Killer Dialogue*. To learn more about Andrea, visit ajthenovelist.com or follow her on Instagram @ajthenovelist.

Dedication

To any writer experiencing self-doubt: The book of your dreams is living on the other side of that fear. Let these words be your guide.

Contents

Introduction 9

What Is Dialogue? 13

> What Is the Purpose of Dialogue? 16

> What Is Bad Dialogue? 19

> Exercise: What Is Dialogue? 29

Creative Non-Fiction 30

Four Types of Dialogue 35

> Direct Dialogue 35

> Indirect Dialogue 36

> Summarized Speech 37

> Internal Dialogue 38

Show, Don't Tell 47

> Exercise: Show, Don't Tell 52

Using Dialogue to Build Character 54

> Creating Distinct Characters 55

> Exercise: Creating Distinct Characters 63

> Goals and Motivation 63

> Exercise: Goals and Motivation 65

Conflict, Tension, and Suspense 66

> Tension **67**

> Suspense **70**

Gestures & Body Language 74

> Exercise: Gestures & Body Language **77**

Subtext 79

> Exercise: Subtext **83**

Silence in Dialogue 84

> Exercise: Silence in Dialogue **85**

The Power of the Pause 86

Humor 89

> Exercise: Humor **98**

Inflammatory Language 102

Historical Language 105

Accents, Dialects, & Foreign Languages 107

> Accents **107**

> Dialects **110**

> Foreign Languages **113**

> Resources: Accents. Dialects, & Foreign Languages **114**

- Exercise: Accents, Dialects, & Foreign Languages **115**
- Slang **116**
- Phone Conversations **118**
- Jargon **121**

Point of View 125

- Exercise: Point of View **127**

Emotion in Dialogue 128

- Mood **129**
- Figurative Language and Symbolism **130**
- Exercise: Figurative Language and Symbolism **131**
- Theme **131**
- Exercise: Theme **132**

Using Dialogue to Propel the Plot 133

- Setting **135**
- Pacing **140**
- Exercise: Pacing **144**
- Time **145**
- Foreshadowing **146**

Exposition 148

- > Maid-and-Butler Dialogue **148**

Structuring a Dialogue Scene 152

Asymmetrical Dialogue 157

Punctuating and Formatting Dialogue 166

- > The Power of Said **167**
- > Adverbs: Let's Talk About Those "-ly" Words **171**
- > Present Participles **173**
- > Dialogue: Formatting Guidelines **176**
- > Exercise: Dialogue Formatting **186**
- > Action Beats **187**

Italics, Dashes, Ellipses, and Hyphens 189

- > Italics **189**
- > Dashes: A Formal Introduction **193**
- > Hyphen **197**
- > Ellipses **198**

I'm Stuck! What Should I Do? 202

Frequently Asked Questions 205

Revision and Editing 216

- > Exercise: Revision and Editing **219**
- > Concision **220**

› Exercise: Concision **228**

› Active v. Passive Voice **229**

Recap and Review 232

Conclusion 237

Author's Note 240

Introduction

Why do characters speak?

Well, it's definitely not conversation for conversation's sake.

Story-based dialogue is more than a person-to-person exchange of information. The characters speak to achieve a goal—the goal of obtaining something from another person through a calculated attack or the goal of protecting and defending something the other person may be trying to take in return. In contrast, real-world dialogue is less precise often built on pleasantries and other meanderings that dilute the effectiveness of the storytelling. Literary dialogue is much tighter and faster and filled with hidden meaning because people are usually speaking not only to convey information but also to receive something from the other person or to enact some social move—whether that's to dominate or ingratiate themselves.

Therefore, writing dialogue is less like speaking and more like composing music. There's a rhythm to how people speak. Shakespeare famously wrote most of his work in iambic pentameter. Of course, you don't need to be that measured, but that's positive proof that audiences enjoy language with rhythm. Just think about the beats and pauses involved in telling a joke. A good comic uses the ebb and flow of the audiences' reactions to time the telling of his tale and establish a musical call-and-response of humor versus laughter, setup versus punchline.

You can do the same with your dialogue even if all you do, at first, is think about things in simple terms of fast or slow, loud and soft. For instance, someone from New York may speak faster and louder than someone from Atlanta. Look for the hills and valleys, the crescendos and decrescendos in the way people talk and how that music changes as they grow angry, sad, excited, or hysterical.

But how do the goals and musicality of dialogue lead to the characterization of each speaker and the relationships between them? Through vital storytelling elements such motivation, conflict, and tension as well as subtext, silence, and humor—all of which work together to help you develop speech patterns that make those characters easily distinguishable.

This book will cover all of those elements in addition to the aspects of dialogue that writers find troubling, such as dialect, slang, jargon, accents, and punctuation—the last of which plays a crucial but significantly underrated role. You'll also discover the difference in usage between an ellipsis (...) and an em dash(—), among other aspects of mechanics. But don't worry! This guide isn't a grammar textbook, so we don't focus on syntax for too long. In fact, feel free to review the table of contents for a more granular list of the topics covered.

Each section offers several examples and practice exercises designed to illustrate and reinforce the concepts covered in the text. Our focus will be on the story elements and formatting techniques of fiction and creative nonfiction writers, but since dialogue is at the heart of all storytelling, many of the concepts may prove helpful to screenwriters and playwrights as well.

In a nutshell, this book will also help you . . .

- Overcome your fears of writing dialogue
- Create characters who sound like real people rather than stereotypes
- Develop your own writing style
- Learn how to format dialogue
- Craft dialogue exchanges that foster conflict, build tension, and drive the plot
- Determine whether you have too much (or not enough!) dialogue

- Produce memorable characters with unique voices and individual styles
- Adopt an effective yet enjoyable approach to writing dialogue

This last point is important. While I want you to gain a solid method for crafting dialogue, the manner in which you go about this endeavor should align with your skills and sensibilities. Obviously, there is an exception to every rule. But if you are lost for an approach, this book offers time-tested advice that, if followed, will result in compelling dialogue.

Now, with that said, I'm not here to dissuade anyone from doing something that has brought them positive results. I am simply interested in making sure your work contains the elements necessary to get fans (and agents!) addicted to your work.

You can read this guide in sections or from beginning to end, but I encourage you to take notes so that the techniques stay with you. In addition, keep in mind that the concepts discussed in this book are filtered through the discussion of dialogue. So naturally, the scope of some topics like tension, suspense, pacing, conflict, and foreshadowing spans beyond the elements discussed here. Therefore, I encourage you to continue researching and practicing once you've finished this book. Pick up a copy of my other reference guide, *Mastering the Art of Suspense*, or join my newsletter for more information. But most importantly, follow up on any supplemental material mentioned, particularly if it remedies one of your weak spots.

I encourage you to embrace the concept of life-long learning because writing, like any other art, has tricky nuances that are always changing. During my publication journey, I took this advice to the extreme by attending graduate school for an MFA in Writing Popular Fiction. Of course, you don't have to go to such lengths (unless you want to), especially since I've already laid the groundwork for you.

So with career growth as our mindset, let's get started. Consider this book my way of sharing what I've learned while getting you excited about your journey and saving you a little time and money along the way. Whether you're a plotter or a pantser, my goal is for you to become passionate about taking your writing to the next level while giving you the tools to craft killer dialogue.

What Is Dialogue?

In the introduction, I promised to make this a lighthearted reference guide that you could read cover to cover or in segments; however, I'd be remiss if I didn't start with a little history to help you better understand why this concept is so important and why I've chosen to highlight some concepts more than others.

First, what is dialogue? Well, according to *Merriam-Webster Dictionary Online*, dialogue comes from the Greek roots *dia–* ("through" or "across") and *–logue* ("discourse" or "talk"). So, think of the basic definition for dialogue as "through discourse" or "an exchange of ideas back-and-forth." In fact, dialogue finds its roots in the Socratic Method, where Socrates would use probing questions to expose his disciples' misconceptions. And yet, it is his most famous student, Plato, who's often given credit for having coined the term "dialogue" (around 4th century B.C.) since Plato authored the earliest known preserved works. Plato's dialogues often placed Socrates in the role of protagonist and are still considered remarkable examinations of man's virtues and vices.

But when it comes to creative writing, I believe we can broaden the definition of dialogue to encompass the spoken (and unspoken) interactions a character has with herself, the reader, or any other entity within the novel—including ghosts, pets, or inanimate objects—as she works to pursue a goal or defend a choice.

In other words, **dialogue is your story's action through discourse**—the verbal actions that outline what a character wants and how they plan to obtain it; the physical actions, such as gesture and body language, that accompany those words; and the thought actions that form the beliefs, expectations, and attitudes behind a character's decision-making process.

And so, today's writers use dialogue to complicate their characters' agendas and propel the plot, but this wasn't always the case.

Consider *Don Quixote* (1605) by Miguel de Cervantes. Many literary critics, such as Anne J. Cruz, Ph.D., coeditor of *Cervantes and His Postmodern Constituencies*, mark *Don Quixote* as one of our first modern novels thanks to its use of different languages, cultures, and views on history through the perspectives of a diverse cast. And yet, if you examine that early entry in our literary canon as well as those that follow (Byron, Shelley, Hawthorne, et cetera), you'll discover that those texts rely heavily on narrative elements rather than dialogue—even the early Greek plays of the 5th century had narrators whereas most of today's plays consist only of dialogue and stage direction.

The shift toward more dialogue-centric fiction began with Charles Dickens, who got his start in serials with *The Pickwick Papers* (1836), published in 19 issues over 20 months. The success of this novel helped popularize serialized fiction, and Dickens found that one of the best ways to hold readers' attention from issue to issue was by focusing on dialogue. Why? Well, dialogue was—and still is—easier for the audience to read, digest, and remember.

These days, action and dialogue are the top elements contemporary authors rely upon to fuel their stories, especially in genre fiction.

Therefore, dialogue must be more than idle conversation.

Good dialogue exposes conflict. Good dialogue reveals character. Good dialogue moves the story forward and places characters in pursuit of their goals. Of course, why the characters are speaking, what each character says, and how they convey that information will ultimately be determined by the context of each scene and the story's genre. But regardless of the situation, in order for the dialogue to prove effective, there must be resistance, tension, and innuendo to keep the action moving in the right direction.

Simply put, good dialogue is vitally important for storytelling.

Dialogue is an effective tool, especially for genre writers, because it is the only part of the manuscript where there is no filter between the audience and the people who inhabit the story. The narrative aspects of description and exposition are gone, and the author allows the characters to guide the action and develop their own voice. Readers enjoy this element of fiction because it makes the characters feel real and is infinitely easier (and more interesting) to read.

If you want to study great dialogue, read the works of Elmore Leonard and Richard Price, who are routinely hailed by contemporary critics as the best writers of crime dialogue. I would also recommend Walter Mosley, Michael Connelly, James Ellroy, Joe R. Landsdale, Janet Evanovich, Patricia Highsmith, Gregory Mcdonald, George V. Higgins, Scott Turow, and John D. MacDonald.

You'll notice my list consists entirely of mystery and thriller writers because that's what I love to read, but you can also find great dialogue in the works of Toni Morrison, Judy Bloom, Audrey Wick, Molly Harper, Terry McMillan, Eric Jerome Dickey, N.K. Jemisin, and many others.

I also recommend studying playwrights since their work relies mostly upon stage directions and direct dialogue, which results in language that's heavy with emotion. Here are some classics to get you started:

- *The Beauty Queen of Leenane* (1996) by Martin McDonagh
- *A Street Car Named Desire* (1947) by Tennessee Williams
- *Bus Stop* (1955) by William Inge
- *Who's Afraid of Virginia Woolf?* (1962) by Edward Albee
- *Glengarry Glen Ross* (1983) by David Mamet

- *Fences* (1985) by August Wilson
- *Topdog/Underdog* (1999) by Suzan-Lori Parks

If you prefer to review screenplays (since they also rely primarily on dialogue and stage directions but for the visual medium), you can find full scripts online through the following websites:

- *Internet Movie Screenplay Database* - https://imsdb.com/
- *Drew's Script-O-Rama* (downloadable PDFs) - http://www.script-o-rama.com/snazzy/table.html
- *Script Slug* (downloadable PDFs) - https://www.scriptslug.com/
- *Awesome Film* - http://www.awesomefilm.com/
- *Screenplays For You* - https://sfy.ru/
- *Simply Scripts* (includes teleplays, musicals, and non-English scripts) - https://www.simplyscripts.com/
- *The Script Lab* (account registration required, recent releases only) - https://thescriptlab.com/

What Is the Purpose of Dialogue?

As noted in the previous section, dialogue is the medium through which characters exchange information and how the reader becomes invested in the story—what a character says or doesn't say helps the audience better understand who they are, what they believe, and what they want. In essence, dialogue is action through discourse, and characters use each exchange to pursue their goals or satisfy conflict, but how does dialogue serve your story overall?

Good dialogue should . . .

- Advance plot
- Develop character (personality, values)

- Illustrate the dynamic between characters
- Mirror themes and foreshadow action
- Amplify tone (attitude) and mood (atmosphere, feeling)
- Enhance settings
- Add conflict, tension, and suspense
- Pique the reader's interest or get them emotionally involved
- Contain higher stakes beneath the words spoken; aka subtext, the dialogue's secondary or underlying level of intention, symbolism, or meaning

Your goal is to craft dialogue that is doing two or more of these at once while also being easy to read and understand. For example, if your protagonist makes a statement that addresses the setting, his description (or the way he chooses to convey it) should also reveal something about his emotions, attitude, or worldview.

In addition, dialogue should entertain, but be careful because that's not the main goal. **First and foremost, we want to create exchanges that serve the story.** However, it can't hurt to develop dialogue that's memorable and gives your audience a thrill, chill, or a chuckle. This book will show you how to do it all.

Dialogue is most effective when it sounds similar to natural speech but without the tangents and chit-chat that act as filler. We also want to provide enough information to clarify the characters' motivations while also being nuanced enough that readers can differentiate among the characters through their word choice and manner of speaking.

Each genre, story, or character will require a particular type of dialogue, and you should write that dialogue so that it is unique to the character you're creating. The setting, tone, and situation will help you to determine what should be said and how it will be delivered. You should not be able to interchange dialogue between characters and have a scene still work. In fact, the characterization created through your dialogue should allow the audience to be able to distinguish characters even if their name or dialogue tags aren't used.

Good dialogue should attack and defend, meaning that it should contribute to the plot by helping your character challenge someone else through inquiry and argument or defend their position through tenacity and perseverance. However, not every conflict needs to be confrontational. For example, friends can disagree about whether a blind date went perfectly or poorly without engaging in a fist fight; that is to say, conflict can take many forms such as protecting one's ego or divulging secrets.

Effective dialogue teaches readers about the human condition and challenges their thinking through the characters' growth and the story's themes—the fragility of ego, the sustainability of love, the commonalities of culture, et cetera. Obviously, books have also become a means of escape where people attempt to immerse themselves in another world or time period, but audiences also want to see parts of themselves reflected back to them. Strong dialogue helps to satisfy those desires by engaging the reader's empathetic nervous system and allowing them to emotionally identify with, or be empowered by, the story in some small way.

So in a nutshell, why is it important to write good dialogue? Dialogue makes the reader feel as if they are part of the story, engaged in the action. And if a reader becomes hooked by your dialogue, they'll probably fall in love with your characters and want to follow them throughout your story. Even if there are areas of your manuscript that still need improvement, great dialogue indicates that you have a solid framework and a clear grasp of what it takes to tell a convincing story—and that's the main thing agents and editors look for when acquiring a book.

What Is Bad Dialogue?

Before we examine each component of good dialogue, let's outline some of the major pitfalls. This may help you better understand why the approach you've used up to this point hasn't given you the results you desire.

CLICHÉS

Clichés are an overused theme, characterization, or situation—or in the case of dialogue, a commonly used phrase or expression. Because we've seen or heard them before, they are highly predictable. Writers often default to clichés because they act as a reliable shorthand that the audience immediately recognizes, making the author's job easier. On the other hand, these cookie-cutter phrases can make it difficult for you to create memorable moments that are specific to the unique characters you've developed.

The best way to produce original dialogue is to create your own idioms and approaches to language. Turn clichés on their head and never opt for the first choice that comes to mind. Generate as many versions of the situation or phrase as possible. Explore the farthest reaches of your characters' personalities to see what wildly innovative material they place on the page. Remember, unpredictable dialogue helps to create change and turn the story. By going the extra mile to create something new, you will not only stretch your writing muscles but also increase the chances that you'll stumble upon that million dollar phrase or outrageous plot twist that your audience will never see coming.

ON-THE-NOSE DIALOGUE

On-the-nose dialogue refers to instances when the characters are saying exactly what they mean and responding to exactly what has been said. This may seem harmless and somewhat logical, but real-world conversations don't work that way and neither should fictional ones. People rarely speak honestly to each other because they are too busy calculating how to push their own agenda.

But more to the point, since on-the-nose writing puts all thoughts and desires on full display, it eradicates any opportunity for subtext and uncertainty to flourish. Remember, good dialogue should breed conflict and tension, but in order to do that, some parts of each character's agenda (goals, motivations, and tactics) should be implied rather than spoken. After all, readers take great joy in unearthing the hidden meaning behind a character's behavior and that additional interaction with the story enriches the audience's experience. By utilizing subtext and avoiding on-the-nose writing, you're more likely to create dialogue that feels authentic to the reader.

On a related note, avoid crafting dialogue where every character knows exactly what the other means—or worse, what the other character is thinking. In the real world, misunderstandings are common because we often form our response before the other person has finished speaking. This can be extremely helpful for the writer whose work should be infused with conflict. So, think about how to create misunderstandings where one character interprets things differently or hears what they want to hear.

For example, one character may say something as simple as *Ugh, pasta again?* However, the other person in the scene may hear that statement and respond to it as if the first character said, *Your cooking sucks!* This misunderstanding creates friction that will make your scene more interesting. Plus, a character's interpretation (or misinterpretation) of a situation tells us a lot about their inner life as well as their relationship with others.

PURPLE PROSE

Purple prose refers to dialogue or description that is ornate, flowery, or melodramatic to the point that it makes the text difficult to take seriously. Such an approach often involves excessive or unearned emotions, run-on sentences, verbosity, and an abundance of clichés. A writer who has fallen into this trap may be using highly poetic or unnecessarily sophisticated language, making it difficult for the reader to understand the intention of the scene. Any conflict that goes from zero to sixty without justification would fall into this category as well.

Be advised that if you're using language that is far more heightened than the emotions demonstrated by your character, you're probably attempting to make too much out of too little. You can easily identify these scenes because they often include too many fully capitalized phrases or an overabundance of italics and exclamation points.

REPEATING CHARATER NAMES

Cut extraneous dialogue like greetings, departures, and other space wasters such as having characters constantly address each other by name when talking one on one. The 1987 film *Fatal Beauty*, starring Whoopi Goldberg as Detective Rizzoli, is a hilarious display of this dialogue faux pas.

RIZZOLI

Mike Marshak? What the hell are you doing here? Didn't I tell you never to come here, Mike Marshak? Dammit, Mike, you're going to get us both killed.

While this approach may seem like a harmless annoyance worth enduring for the sake of establishing who is speaking to whom, the added verbiage makes the passage sound idiotic and contrived. Rizzoli clearly has no reason for repeating Mike's full name other than wanting to flag it for the audience. Trust that the reader is paying attention. After all, in addition to hearing the characters use each other's names in speech, the reader also experiences them as part of the dialogue attributions. So if you've formatted your exchanges correctly, the audience should have no problem identifying each character.

Some writers conflate this technique with sincerity or intensity, hoping that the consistent exchange of names will signal to the audience that the dialogue is important or that the characters have encountered a serious problem worthy of the reader's undivided attention. Unfortunately, the repetition has the adverse effect. The audience is annoyed, perhaps even skipping passages, because they've been given information they don't need at a moment when the story should be narrowing its focus.

Be strategic in your use of a character's name. Naturally, your manuscript feels incomplete without them, but this element can be relegated to specific points within a dialogue exchange:

- **When the audience is initially introduced to a character or reintroduced to a character after a long break or when people are meeting each other for the first time.** "I am Gunnery Sergeant Hartman, your senior drill instructor. From now on you will speak only when spoken to, and the first and last words out of your filthy sewers will be 'sir.' Do you maggots understand that?" *Full Metal Jacket* (1987)
- **To gain someone's attention, especially in a crowd or at a distance.** "I want to say one thing to my wife who's home. Yo, Adrian! I did it!" *Rocky* (1976)
- **As an expression of sympathy or to soften the blow of bad news.** "You looking for sympathy, Leo? Look in the dictionary between 'shit' and 'syphilis.'" *Johnny Be Good* (1988)
- **As an expression of anger or exasperation toward a situation, person, or life in general.** "Someday we might

look back on this and decide that saving Private Ryan was the one decent thing we were able to pull out of this whole godawful shitty mess." *Saving Private Ryan* (1988)
- **To denote the end of a conversation or the departure of a character from the story.** "All right, Mr. DeMille, I'm ready for my closeup." *Sunset Boulevard* (1950)
- **To punctuate an important idea, particularly one that illuminates the story's theme.** "Oh, Auntie Em, there's no place like home." *The Wizard of Oz* (1939)

On the other hand, names are a fast way to indicate the level of acquaintance between two characters. We may call someone Mrs. Lopez because we just met them or as a sign of respect because they are older or an authority figure. Someone we call Jennifer might be an acquaintance or coworker of equal status. Shortening that to Jen may show a longstanding relationship as would a nickname like JLo. Nicknames also have the special distinction of allowing insight into personality or appearance. Think about ones like Tiny or Shorty.

Nevertheless, I urge you to use direct address only when it's necessary. As you edit your manuscript, pare down the use of names as a way to help the dialogue sound and feel more natural.

USELESS REPETITION

Avoid repetition. Make sure your characters aren't saying the same things in different ways (or saying different things but using the same speech patterns). There is no need to repeat information unless it is to emphasize a specific point or remind the audience of a past event. In those instances, especially if one character needs to restate an idea that has been covered in detail earlier in the story, it is best to use summary speech.

On a related note, do not use dialogue to exchange information a character already knows. This is called maid-and-butler dialogue, and it often sounds unnatural or forced to the reader. Remember, good fiction conversations should show (not tell) the emotional state of characters and their situations.

With that in mind, it could be argued that dialogue isn't the best mode for conveying exposition as that's usually what a writer is attempting to do when they have characters engaging in maid-and-butler dialogue. Instead, use narrative elements like internal dialogue or direct thought to show how the characters feel about a situation. Or if your novel is written in a more distant viewpoint, simply have the narrator give a brief summary or overview.

Lastly, avoid having your characters talk about wanting to do something then showing them doing it because that's redundant. Simply show the action because it is a more compelling way of depicting the scene.

INFORMATION DUMPS

Information dumping is the act of bombarding the audience with a ton of information at once. This occurs when the narrative pauses to provide the reader with an overabundance of description or backstory over the course of several paragraphs or pages rather than spreading out the information so the details are only revealed when needed. For example:

> "Don't you get it, Linda? I had to protect you. The two of us are all we've got. We've known each other all our lives. You're my older sister, after all. We shared a room all through high school—same clothes, same music, same men. I'll never forget that semester we both dyed our hair platinum blonde to look more like each other. Oh, and remember that guy? What's his name? Raul? The one who kept stealing money

from your wallet? Boy, did he pull the wool over your eyes. I had to slash his tires, so he'd leave you alone. And even then, you went crawling back."

Even out of context, the paragraph feels clunky and superfluous because the reader doesn't have a grasp of the story's characters or their motivations. Sure, we're learning something about the sisters, but is it relevant? Does it drive the plot? The character is talking simply to provide background rather than engaging in a scene based on conflict and her personal agenda.

We want to avoid this in our writing because it lacks tension and involves telling rather than showing. This technique also commits the cardinal sins of sounding random and amateurish while being boring and long-winded. Using dialogue to convey exposition is generally ineffective because we always want our characters, whether friends or foe, to engage in contentious exchanges where they challenge the status quo and protect themselves against physical or emotional damage. We also want our scenes to have layers of meaning. Unfortunately, lengthy explanations lack such nuance.

If you must use dialogue to deliver exposition, make sure the information plays an active role in the exchange. One technique is to embed the background information inside a point of contention or conflict because this produces tension, allows for subtext where the participants may conceal their motives, and develops characterization based on how the players choose to challenge or defend their respective positions. Consider this revised sample:

> My sister looked under the door of each stall then whirled around to face me. "Why the hell is there a cop in my office?"
>
> "Don't act so shocked. I'm trying to protect you."

> "How? By landing me in jail?"
>
> "By doing what I always do—cleaning up your mess. Your deadbeat boyfriend isn't anything but a bigger badder version of Raul from high school, using you for your money. You're just too dumb to see it."
>
> "That didn't mean you had to kill him." Her panic echoed off the bathroom tiles.
>
> "What should I have done? Slashed his tires, so you could feel guilty about it and go running back to him?"

Overall, it's better if you simply relay the information to the audience directly using the narrative voice. To avoid info dumping, you can have one character make a statement to the point-of-view character, which reminds him or her of a crucial background event. Whereupon, the viewpoint character can have a short internal monologue to flesh out the details of that situation. This will give the audience the exposition they need to understand the relationship (strained, bitter, romantic, competitive, et cetera) between the two characters without creating contrived dialogue. This also helps to focus your inclusion of backstory to one or two relevant (and brief!) elements.

Let's look at the scene again. This time we'll use the narrative voice:

> I hated seeing my older sister under the thumb of yet another douchebag. Even though she was five years older, it didn't seem to make her any wiser. Some people have a bad picker, but Linda was simply addicted to the drama. First, there was Raul, the thief. Matt, the booze hound. And now Elliot, a man who not only used her law firm's capital as his personal ATM but who also beat her every time she'd suggest he start a business of his own. Did this mean I took joy in slitting El-

liot's throat? Maybe. But that wasn't the point. I couldn't let another man suck the life out of the only family I had left.

You always want to ensure your writing is a tight balance of forward story action, character development, worldbuilding, and background. The information you choose to include in your dialogue and narrative, whether action or exposition, needs to serve a purpose.

In short, bad dialogue often disturbs the story's reality by being rushed and poorly organized with irrelevant content and awkward transitions that fail to produce a cohesive exchange. You can almost always recognize these scenes because they lack conflict and they fail to focus on what's important about the situation—the character's goals and the stakes they produce. The scene may also move helter-skelter from fact to fact or emotion to emotion without providing a natural buildup, which of course leads to unrealistic reactions from the characters in the scene. This often occurs because the author is prioritizing their desire to create a certain effect or convey their writerly agenda rather than working to match the appropriateness of the moment.

The pitfall most writers fall into is that they think dialogue doesn't require the same forethought as character and story development. On the contrary, all three are inextricably intertwined. If you're struggling to create dialogue, you should take a closer look at how you've structured the scene. Have you started the action in the right place? Are the goals and motivations of your characters clear? Is there something at stake? What's the conflict? Have you given us enough information to understand why the scene matters to the characters, and the overall narrative, without going overboard? What's the subtext?

Remember, it's impossible to conjure strong dialogue from a feeble narrative.

AUTHENTIC DIALOGUE

Fun fact: In real life, most people don't speak in complete sentences and rarely finish their thoughts. Don't believe me? Listen to your friends. The average conversation is a cornucopia of run-on sentences, muddled phrases, false starts, malapropisms, and repetition. Of course, this is amplified when the parties are anxious or emotional. In those instances, the language becomes irrational, rambling, and incoherent. Sometimes these exchanges are profound, but more often than not they're annoying, mundane, or incomprehensible.

So as much as we may want to capture the essence of daily life in our dialogue, an attempt to faithfully recreate such halting and sporadic speech patterns would ruin the forward momentum and overall cohesiveness of our stories. Of course, we want our characters to sound vibrant and spontaneous, but my point is that dialogue isn't meant to be wholly authentic. The language we use in our fiction and screenplays is stylized to reflect realism without being a slave to it. When there are moments of non-sequitur or tangential dialogue in the narrative, they feel real only because the author eventually finds a way for that information to serve the scene in terms of characterization, exposition, or subtext. Everything we write should be honed to be compelling, entertaining, and informative.

Bottomline: Dialogue is wittier and more focused than real life. **Every word must have a purpose.**

Unfortunately, in real life, people rarely speak their minds. So as listeners, we don't always know what's driving their behavior. However, as a writer, you must have a grasp on how your characters convey their emotions and craft their dialogue so the reader understands as well.

Use dialogue, facial expressions, and body language to unveil your characters to the audience. Allow their words to expose their feelings about themselves, their values, their environment, and their peers. This will help drive the plot and clarify the theme. And don't be afraid to put their actions and words at odds because that invites subtext and creates tension for the story as they struggle to achieve their goals.

With that in mind, let's get started.

Exercise: What Is Dialogue?

Exercise: As discussed earlier in this chapter, dialogue is a stylized version of reality. However, everyday speech patterns can still be helpful in developing your characterizations. Observe the world around you and seek to learn the different tactics people use when they're feeling emotional. What gestures and body language do they call upon when they're giddy, nervous, upset, et cetera? How do clothing, shoes, props, and accessories affect status, personality, behavior, or speech patterns? How do people use silence? Are there turns of phrase that strike you as profound? Keep all of your discoveries in a special notebook. You'll find it helpful to refer back to some of these ideas when you write. As an additional exercise, I challenge you to record portions of a normal conversation and rewrite it. Replace things like cliché and exposition with conflict and subtext.

Creative Non-Fiction

What is creative non-fiction? True stories, personal tales, lived experiences, and perceptions. In other words, expository or narrative writing that adopts a creative approach. Think memoirs, blogs, humorous essays, literary journalism, entertainment articles, or topical writing such as nature, travel, food, et cetera.

According to an article by Dinty W. Moore in Issue 56 of *CNF Quarterly*, the earliest use of the term "creative non-fiction" can be found in David Madden's review of Frank Conroy's 1967 memoir, *Stop-Time*. "In the review, which can be found in the 1969 *Survey of Contemporary Literature*, Madden calls for a 'redefinition' of non-fiction writing in the wake of Truman Capote, Jean Stafford, and Norman Mailer . . ."—all of whom were engaging in a new form of journalism that combined the subjective elements of the creative imagination with the more objective qualities of standard reporting.

So in this instance, the "creative" aspect doesn't mean fabricating events or exaggerating. It simply refers to non-fiction writers actively using literary techniques—like characterization, plot, and figurative language—to make their stories more engaging. The term "non-fiction" refers to the fact that these stories focus on real people and real events.

Therefore, since creative non-fiction is grounded in fact, as opposed to fantasy and falsehoods, many authors in this genre avoid using dialogue for fear that it will dilute the veracity of their story. However, dialogue and quoted speech are powerful literary tools that can benefit creative non-fiction writers in a number of ways. Consider these examples:

Direct quotes and dialogue place the reader at the center of the action. Imagine a news story about a devasting house fire that includes a brief interview with the owner. He tells us about what he experienced during the blaze, including how his family narrowly escaped and how all of their belongings were destroyed. Through his statement, the reader better understands the situation and its long-range effects. As an audience, we want to help, and we imagine what we would have done in the same situation. In essence, his speech holds our attention and pulls us into the narrative.

When crafting non-fiction, it's always best to allow for moments when the inhabitants of the story can express themselves. After all, they are essentially your characters, so the more they interact with the reader, the more interesting your tale will become. This also helps your writing stand out from other work that's covering the same topic. And since you're working to create a realistic depiction that's strong enough to engage the reader, you're free to select the most memorable ideas, images, or phrases to recreate the event's mood and tone.

Moreover, even if you're acting as an objective news reporter, direct quotes (from an eyewitness or related sources) can help to capture the various opinions or perspectives on an issue, thereby further exploring the topic, without breaking your role as the neutral party.

Dialogue and direct quotes infuse the narrative with powerful emotions. When characters directly display their emotions and attitudes, the impact is much more significant than narrative description. Remember, dialogue is the primary way to show rather than tell. By permitting your characters to speak their minds or convey a personal experience, you're humanizing the story.

This is an especially powerful storytelling tool for humorous essays and biographies. For example, Will Smith's self-titled memoir, *Will*, opens with an introductory passage simply labeled "The Wall." We're introduced to a young Smith who has been tasked by his father to rebuild an old wall (with the help of his brother) for their family storefront.

The story is meant to illustrate Smith's strained relationship with his father as well as teach a valuable lesson about perseverance. With that in mind, I would argue that it's the various uses of dialogue that make this passage so memorable. First, the audience is given insight into Smith's internal thoughts about this event both as a pre-teen and an adult. Second, we are given lines of dialogue from the young Smith as he explains the absurdity of the situation. And lastly, if not most importantly, we are given direct lines from his father in a gruff tone designed to conjure the moment so that the reader can feel the power of Daddio's stern wisdom.

Review this excerpt from *Will* (2021) by Will Smith with Mark Manson.

> One day, Harry and I were in a particularly stank mood. We were dragging our feet and grumbling, "impossible this" and "ridiculous that."
>
> "Why'd we have to build a wall for, anyway? This is impossible. It's never gonna get done."
>
> Daddio overheard us, threw down his tools, and marched over to where we were yapping. He snatched a brick out of my hand and held it up in front of us.
>
> "Stop thinking about the damn wall!" he said. "There *is* no wall. There are only *bricks*. Your job is to lay *this brick* perfectly. Then move on to the next brick. Then lay *that brick* perfectly. Then the next one. Don't be worrying about no wall. Your only concern is *one brick*."
>
> He walked back into the shop. Harry and I looked at each other, shook our heads—*This dude's a kook*—and went back to mixing.

Is that exactly what his father said in that moment? Maybe, maybe not. But if you're fixated on that, you're missing the point. To impart the lesson effectively, the scene needed to be created with setting, characterization, motivation, tension, and *dialogue*. Obviously, the writer wants to stick as close to what was said as possible. However, there is some dramatic license to present the scene in a way where the purpose and consequences are clear to the reader.

Use your best recollection, or simply the essence of a moment, to craft dialogue that turns a partial memory into a full scene. This will allow you to draft a cohesive story with characters, a forward-moving storyline, and a lesson or theme. If you're stuck on what to use and what to avoid, consider what message you want to highlight and what impact those words have on everyone involved (both inside and outside the story). And of course, your dialogue should accurately reflect the personality of the speaker as well as the time and place. Trust that when you recall a past event, the reader understands that you may not have captured the exact words spoken, but you have captured the true intention behind the moment. As long as you remain consistent with your depictions, you're also free to add gestures, thoughts, and action to enhance your non-fiction dialogue.

Direct quotes and dialogue make for powerful opening lines. Every story should start with an idea, image, concept, or moment of change that grabs the audience's attention and entices them to keep reading. In genre fiction, this is known as a hook. In journalism, this is called putting your headlining information above the fold. But the point is that when you use dialogue or direct quotes to open your work, it permits the article or essay to begin like a story. As noted in the previous passage, people are drawn to personal anecdotes. They are a striking way to introduce difficult or controversial concepts—especially if you want to garner audience support or inspire action (as with books on weight loss, mental health, et cetera). Don't be afraid to utilize personal stories or humanizing quotes throughout the text to illustrate new concepts, shift the tone, or exemplify your theme.

Bottomline: Dialogue and direct quotes can be a helpful tool for nonfiction writers when used responsibly. Just make sure the speeches or characterizations you choose to incorporate support the story's purpose and advance the narrative.

Four Types of Dialogue

Even though the goal of this book is to give you a broader definition for dialogue, I believe it is fair to say that most people would define the term, on its most basic level, as *speech* or *the words spoken aloud by characters*. However, if we think of dialogue solely in those terms, its use and scope is extremely limited.

But when considering the various ways we must approach language in order to build characters, tension, and the plot, it's far more productive to define dialogue as *a method of conveying the story's action* and *one of the crucial keys to conflict*. Consider dialogue as *words in action* with others, oneself, and the audience. In each case, this speech action moves the characters toward their goals and drives the story.

With that in mind, this chapter is devoted to helping you see that dialogue can take four main forms and that they should be used in various combinations to give your characters depth, vary the pacing, and drive the story.

Direct Dialogue

Direct dialogue refers to the words spoken aloud by the characters as represented by the words placed inside quotation marks. Dialogue reads faster than narrative and audiences pay more attention to it because they get to experience the action of the scene or the reactions to an event in real time.

> EXAMPLE: "You look lovely," Ethan said. "May I buy you a drink?"

- Good for hooking audience interest
- Good for showing character reactions

- Good for breaking up staid narrative and slow pacing
- Good for advancing the plot
- Good for developing character
- Good for setting the scene
- Good for establishing conflict and tension

When crafting new dialogue, you're writing to propel the action of the current scene, but you also need to consider the characters' prior actions to understand WHY the conversation is taking place. You also need to be cognizant of HOW these words will guide, shift, or setup the story to come.

Indirect Dialogue

Indirect dialogue, sometimes referred to as *reported speech*, occurs when the narrator paraphrases a speaker's dialogue or intention, rather than directly quoting them. In essence, the author cloaks pieces of dialogue within the narrative to give the essence of what was said without incorporating the actual words used during the exchange.

> EXAMPLE: Ethan complimented my dress then asked me to join him at the bar for a drink.

- Good for relaying background or exposition
- Good for denoting a minor passage of time or compressing real-time events
- Good for conveying interactions that are needed for clarity but don't need to be specifically dwelled upon (like greetings and closers)

Indirect dialogue requires the reader to imagine the exchange while direct dialogue uses the personalized dramatizations of the character. Keep this in mind when deciding which form provides the best impact for your scene. Audiences tend to remember and relate to direct dialogue for longer periods, so a direct exchange may prove more effective if you want to emphasize an event or highlight a clue.

Summarized Speech

Summarized speech is used to provide a brief synopsis of what characters have said without going into major detail. This occurs when the scope of that information is too large or perhaps not relevant enough to convey as direct or indirect speech. Authors also use summarized speech when the information being conveyed has already been relayed as action or direct dialogue and does not need to be repeated.

> EXAMPLE: After an hour of flirting over some greasy Chinese takeout, he finally made his move.

Note in this example, we don't get any specific mentions of how he flirted or what he said. Unlike indirect dialogue, summarized speech doesn't need to be as specific. The goal is simply to advance the story as efficiently as possible.

Summarized speech is best utilized when you want to acknowledge the effect of a long exchange without reproducing it verbatim. This is often used during transitions (e.g. summarizing the airport security check as a quick cut to the next scene) or when the author has a character repeating information the audience already knows—rather than reusing the same dialogue from scene to scene, the author summarizes the conversation.

You can also use summarized speech to compress information that doesn't need to be explained in detail or may not be as crucial to the present scene as other material. However, avoid using this technique as the bulk of every scene because you will create a boring story that fails to capture reader interest.

EXAMPLE: After school, Mary told her sister about her day—the substitute in homeroom, the food fight at lunch, and getting an A+ on her math exam—but she carefully avoided describing the fun she had in study hall passing notes with Jake because she knew her twin would be jealous.

In this example, the gist of the interaction is delivered through summarized speech. The transition along with the combination of events alludes to a passage of time and provides significant plot advancement by referencing a full conversation without burdening the reader with all the boring stuff.

- Good for transitions between scenes
- Good for denoting a major passage of time
- Good for relaying background or exposition
- Good for moving quickly through a big event or a series of events
- Good for avoiding repetition
- Good for regulating pace

Internal Dialogue

Internal dialogue includes the thoughts or inner voice of a character when they speak to themselves or the audience. In this instance, the quotation marks are removed to make it clear the words are occurring inside someone's head. Dialogue tags are also unnecessary.

You may sometimes see such speech represented by italics; however, the current trend is to maintain plain text and allow the internal dialogue to evolve through context.

Be advised that since a character's thoughts are often dramatized as an inner struggle between two sides of the same being, all internal monologues should be classified as internal dialogue, especially when it is in conflict with what they are saying aloud or how they are behaving. On that note, throughout the book I may sometimes slip and refer to this category as internal monologue, which could lead some people to believe that I consider each character's inner musings a solo or static endeavor.

Rest assured, I am well aware that our thoughts are often a crisscrossing discourse—(*dia-* "through" and *-logue* "talk")—i.e. a mish-mash of voices that represent the weight of the world, the opinions of our parents, the peer pressure from our friends as well as our own values, opinions, fears, and idiosyncrasies. Thus, I support the idea (and you should too) that internal dialogue and internal monologue can be used interchangeably when referring to the personal statements that form inside our characters' heads.

With that said, avoid allowing your characters' internal monologues to turn into information dumps. These musings should be a direct reflection of what's currently happening in the story through the filter of the character's personality.

> EXAMPLE: I glance over to find Larry staring at the blood on my collar. Shit. Breathe. Be cool. Admit nothing.

- Good for connecting with the audience
- Good for establishing a character's personality and growth
- Good for understanding a character's emotional state
- Good for demonstrating a character's motivations and desires
- Good for contrasting the difference between a character's actions and beliefs
- Good for relaying background or exposition
- Good for transitioning from subject to subject
- Good for establishing conflict and tension

Keep in mind, if your story is in the first-person viewpoint, the overall narrative is filtered through the character's thoughts. Therefore, any statement the viewpoint character makes to themselves outside of the quotation marks is considered internal dialogue. In such instances, you don't need italics or the addition of *I thought*, *I wondered*, or *I pondered*. To use those indicators suggests the narrator is different from the character and, again, in first person that's not the case.

> As I strolled down the stairway, Trevor caught my gaze and winked. He was finally flirting with me, ~~I thought~~. Thank God he noticed me over Bianca.

Notice the entire passage, including the inner voice, is in first person, past tense. Of course, since the narrative and the character's thoughts are intertwined in that past tense, you may not have very much material that feels spontaneous, but the flirtation and the relief, as noted in the above example, still count toward the character thinking to themselves.

The great thing is that this approach also works in third person. In fact, you may see some authors italicizing lines to emphasize the character's thoughts. But if you're writing a close third person, italics aren't necessary since the goal is to seamlessly show the audience what the character is experiencing and feeling through the unseen narrator. Even in third person, to point out a character's emotions with italics breaks the illusion of being directly involved with the person in the story. Here is an example of incorporating internal dialogue in close third.

> As Juanita strolled down the staircase, Trevor caught her gaze and winked. Finally! He was flirting with her. Thank God he'd noticed her over Bianca.

Once again, the entire passage, including the inner voice is in third person and maintains the past tense to create a unified narrative.

Now, of course, this approach will not work with third person objective where the whole point of that type of narration is to convey the action without moving into the mind of any specific character. And it may also provide difficult for third person omniscient since the narrator is rarely linked to a specific character. Moreover, omniscient viewpoint often carries a substantial psychic distance, which is how near or far your audience feels to the person or entity telling the story.

So with omniscient viewpoint, it occasionally makes sense to add the *she thought* indicator to let us know that a specific character is having an internal moment. You can also use italics if you prefer, but **you don't need to do both** because you would be doubling up on what's considered two sides to the same technique. Remember, the entire purpose of both the *she thought* tag and the italics is to provide a way of indicating internal monologue.

But again, the current trend is to avoid italics and tags so that the internal dialogue flows seamlessly into the narrative. This keeps the audience anchored into the story. Here is another example of how to do it best, using a semi-omniscient approach:

> As Bianca strolled down the staircase, Trevor caught her gaze and winked. He was finally flirting, and she smiled a little brighter knowing he'd noticed her over Bianca.

Even though internal dialogue is a powerful tool for conveying information, it is important to remember that it's not the only way to advance the plot or develop characters. In fact, each time the story stops to go into someone's mind, you're pausing the action and diverting the plot, so don't rely entirely on thoughts. Work to create a balance of internal musings and external exchanges. The variation keeps your audience from getting bored and ensures a well-paced narrative.

On a related note, avoid having the characters talk aloud to themselves or to their pets, which is not only cliché but also limiting. Without a secondary being to engage in the exchange, the dialogue falls flat due to the lack of conflict and tension. It's better to have the character grapple with the problem internally where their ego, doubt, and insecurities will act as the scene's opposition.

And of course, don't forget to stay consistent throughout the narrative with whatever technique you're using so the audience never has a problem understanding what you're attempting to do.

DIRECT THOUGHTS

However, if you want to incorporate the immediate, intimate thoughts of a character (often referred to as **direct thoughts**), you should take a slightly different approach. Notice how the following passage uses the present tense to subtly incorporate the character's real-time thoughts.

> As I strolled down the staircase, Trevor caught my gaze and winked. Is he finally flirting with me? Surely, I'm dreaming.

Review the next section. This example of direct thoughts not only switches from past to present tense but also moves from third to first viewpoint.

> As Juanita strolled down the staircase, Trevor caught her gaze and winked. Is he finally flirting with me? Surely, I'm dreaming.

While these may feel like the preferred way to write all internal dialogue, the unannounced changes in tense or point of view may confuse your audience if you overdo it. Instead, use direct thoughts strategically and sparingly. After all, this is ultimately a technique about *emphasis* since it uses literary devices to separate thought from the narrative.

Basically, this approach works best in high-stakes situations where your character is a conveying an important emotion or idea that will help turn the story or provide a vital clue.

And yes, in terms of emphasis, direct thoughts have the added benefit of creating a slight contrast between the narrative action (what a character does) versus what the character thinks and feels—a great reflection of how humans face conflict and contradiction in real life. But as noted earlier in this chapter, there are many other ways to do this so that narrative and thoughts flow together seamlessly. We shouldn't want to alter the structure and tense of our story unless the plot or characterization demands we do so.

Furthermore, you should avoid presenting all of your characters' thoughts as a series of rhetorical questions. For example:

> I stared into his eyes for a sign. Should I trust him? And if I do, how do I keep from getting hurt? Or is that fact alone enough to doubt him?

While this approach may appear to increase tension and emphasize the gravity of a character's dilemma, the overuse of questions actually dumbs down the story by telling the reader what they should be focusing upon rather than allowing them to draw their own conclusions. In other words, it is an obvious way for the author to intrude upon the narrative to say, "Consider this, dear reader."

Plus, rhetorical questions often repeat information in a manner that makes the character seem indecisive. Nobody likes a waffler. So do your story a favor, give your players enough autonomy to address their emotions and make clear decisions—good or bad. This makes them more relatable to the reader and shows you've done the hard work of understanding how they'll react to almost any situation. Not to mention, decisions that result in direct action open the door to further conflict, which is the foundation of great storytelling.

Remember, keep it simple. Lose the rhetorical questions. Allow your character to describe the situation, mull over the issue, and devise an answer. Trust that your adept storytelling has already piqued the audience's curiosity about the problem at hand. Consider this update:

> I stared into his eyes for a sign. A flash of warmth. Some softening around the edges. A twinkle of guilt—something to let me know that he remembered why we fell in love. But there was none of it. Everything that washed over me was cold, steely, and unyielding. He couldn't be trusted.

Overall, be careful with internal dialogue because we never want to pull our audience out of the story during our attempts to use it. The less skilled we are when introducing a character's internal dialogue, the more likely the audience will be aware of the psychic distance between the narrator and the character, which may diminish their enjoyment and your credibility as a writer.

STREAM OF CONSCIOUNESS

Stream of consciousness is another approach to internal dialogue that attempts to break down the barriers between the audience and the players, allowing the reader deep inside the viewpoint character's perspective. This approach presents those thoughts (usually in first and/or second-person viewpoint) as they exist before the mind has edited, punctuated, or arranged them into coherent sentences. The goal is to reveal the character's consciousness in a truly realistic manner.

You may hear some people refer to this technique as free association because it is meant to mimic the non-linear nature of the human brain. Writers who opt for this approach want to expose the character's psychological truth and give the audience the impression that the character, not the author, has sole control of the narrative. Think of this as the literary equivalent of breaking the fourth wall so the audience is fully involved.

This method has been used by a number of notable writers such as Virginia Woolf, James Joyce, William Faulkner, Marcel Proust, Henry James, Leo Tolstoy, Sylvia Plath, Jack Kerouac, and Toni Morrison. According to *Encyclopedia Britannica Online*, psychologist William James first used the term in *The Principles of Psychology* (1980) to describe our incessant flow of thoughts. Basically, stream of consciousness delves into the far reaches of the mind to illustrate the character's authentic self without interference or commentary from the author.

What's important to remember about stream of consciousness is that it's not as consistent as internal dialogue. That is to say, even though both have the advantage of taking the reader inside the character's mind, stream of consciousness is unorganized, uncensored, and unpredictable. Again, it is meant to be a realistic reflection of a character's perceptions without any interference from the author or the story's narrative push. However, that approach sometimes results in material that's incohesive and therefore less accessible to the audience.

We don't usually see stream of consciousness in commercial fiction because genre writers want their characters' thoughts to be relatable, accessible, and legible to the reader. In other words, authors of popular fiction want the internal monologue uniform enough that—even if we alter the viewpoint to second person to highlight the inner talk or switch to the present tense to create immediacy—the audience clearly understands what the character is mulling over, why those thoughts are important, and how those thoughts may influence the story moving forward. Genre writers are always careful about only including information that's relevant to driving the plot forward toward the conclusion.

If you're interested in learning more about stream of consciousness, here's a short list of literary examples to explore:

- *Night* (1972) by Edna O'Brien
- *On the Road* (1957) by Jack Kerouac
- *Mrs. Dalloway* (1925) by Virginia Woolf
- *Ulyssess* (1922) by James Joyce

You can also tap into your own stream of consciousness by simply journaling everything that goes through your mind for five or ten minutes. Getting in touch with how people think may help you to better convey that experience in your work.

Show, Don't Tell

Show, don't tell is a reminder that good storytelling should strive for dynamic dramatization, rather than passive explanation.

To show is to present a situation using sensory details, characters, actions, emotions, and dialogue. Showing drives the story and immerses the reader in the setting as if they're there with the characters. This approach expands the characterization and allows the reader to draw conclusions about what's happening based on the characters' motivations and desires.

To tell is to rely on explanation rather than action. Characterizations and events are summarized rather than dramatized. Sure, telling can be used to set a scene, but the results are distant and sluggish. Ultimately, telling fails to develop compelling imagery, emotion, and subtext, which blocks the audience's access to the characters' inner lives.

Here are several ways to *show, don't tell* more effectively:

Through dialogue. "Don't worry." I stroked his scabby head until the mewing was replaced by a faint purr. "Everything will be okay."

Through actions. I tucked the kitten under my jacket and ran out of the woods.

Through thoughts. What kind of filthy human leaves a precious kitten out here to die? This is exactly why I can't stand being around people.

Through comparisons. "Good thing I came alone this time." I whispered as the kitten purred. "Otherwise, my sisters might have decided you'd be good practice for their slingshots."

Through narrative description. The kitten was a scrawny thing with burrs and bits of wood caught in its hair and the milky white pus of neglect coming out of its eyes and nose.

Notice that the techniques listed here include action, dialogue, and narrative.

Physical action provides the story with movement.

Dialogue is the story's action put into thoughts and words—whether that's the character's internal struggle or an exchange between two or more characters. Direct dialogue and thoughts are immediate. Most of the time, these exchanges reflect the present moment even when they're conveyed in past tense. Narration doesn't have that sense of immediacy; it wallows in explanation and approaches every situation with a broader lens, which results in descriptions that have the power to transcend time and space.

Remember, narrative can introduce characters, illuminate setting, reveal history, display thoughts, flash forward into the future or backward into the past, summarize events, and highlight a theme. And even though narrative leans more toward telling, while dialogue and action favor showing, there's time and place for them all. Ideally, we want to weave the three together to create a picture that's akin to the variety and unpredictability of real life.

So, what's the best ratio?

The answer involves some experimentation and varies based on the intention for each scene and the story's genre. But generally speaking, you never want to go too far in one direction. For example, a scene with an overabundance of dialogue can feel like a group of emotionless talking heads in an empty room. That's definitely a situation that requires some narrative like setting details and physical action such as references to gestures and facial expressions.

If you're lost as to how or where to add this information, put yourself into the mindset of your viewpoint character. Imagine how'd she react to each line of dialogue. Will some lines make her laugh? Will others make her self-conscious? What does she observe about the environment?

And when it comes to how much or how little of this to include, keep in mind that any narrative added to the scene will slow the pace. So for your descriptive elements, look for places where you need to highlight an emotion or lengthen a reaction. Avoid those areas where tension is mounting or action is unfolding at a fast clip. Those moments call for action or dialogue.

So, reevaluate any scene where you've only used one of the essential elements—dialogue, action, and narrative. Consider whether the events feel realistic. Is the pacing right? Does the scene feel dynamic? Are the characters, settings, and actions clear? Is anything missing? Add the absent elements as needed so the three approaches are working together.

FINDING THE SWEET SPOT

Consider these tips for successfully weaving dialogue, action, and narrative into your story.

- If the pace of a scene is lagging or you have too much narrative, add dialogue.
- If you have too much dialogue, add narrative.
- If your characters are sitting around thinking too much, add action.
- If you want to incorporate some background information about the characters to make them more relatable, use narrative and dialogue.

EXCEPTIONS TO THE RULE

Obviously, there will be moments when it is best for one element to dominate over the others. This often occurs during a scene's climax because that's when the pace needs to be amped up for a confrontation or slowed down to unpack a revelation.

For example, you wouldn't want to interrupt the back-and-forth banter of a heated argument to explain what someone is wearing. On the flip side, a chase scene will require mostly action and very little dialogue.

Another reason you may want to focus on a single element is if you need to create a literary closeup on a specific character trait, like a young boy's fear. Your goal is to keep the scene lean and the reader focused. Consider this scene from *The Shining* (1977) by Stephen King:

> Danny looked around the corner.
>
> The fire extinguisher was there, a flat hose folded back a dozen times on itself, red tank attached to the wall. Above it was an axe in a glass case like a museum exhibit, with white words painted on a red background: IN CASE OF EMERGENCY, BREAK GLASS. Danny could read the word EMERGENCY, which was also the name of one of his favorite TV shows, but was unsure of the rest. But he didn't like the way the word was used in connection with that long flat hose. Emergency was fire, explosions, car crashes, hospitals, sometimes death. And he didn't like the way that hose hung there so blandly on the wall. When he was alone, he always skittered past these extinguishers as fast as he could. No particular reason. It just felt better to go fast. It felt safer.

Because this portion of the scene focuses primarily on narrative description, we gain a fuller understanding of Danny's fear and how it manifests in his daily routine.

Bottomline: Even with these exceptions in mind, the overall goal is balance. And if you choose to have a scene with one element, be honest with yourself about whether that choice is working effectively for your story.

STARTING YOUR SCENE

There is much debate about whether it is wise to open a scene with a line of direct dialogue. I am in the camp that thinks it's possible especially if you immediately weave that dialogue with some action, thought, and narrative. But regardless of which side of the argument you favor, the key to starting your scene is to start the dialogue (or action, narrative, et cetera) in the right place.

Start as close as to the point of conflict as possible. Avoid filler which often takes the form of things like personal greetings, discussions about the weather, empty actions that don't serve the scene (like buying a coffee), or lengthy pleasantries with background characters who play no role in the plot. Start your scenes in medias res (i.e. in the middle of things). This can even be mid-conversation as long as the context is clear.

Here are some guidelines for opening your scene strong using the three essential elements. Feel free to execute them in any order, but make sure the start of your scene covers them all.

- Establish the setting
- Create a point of conflict (physical, verbal, or mental)
- Place a conversation starter somewhere in the first two paragraphs
- Ensure the viewpoint character is involved in the conversation (direct or internal)
- Be clear about who is speaking to whom

Bottomline: You certainly want to get into the dialogue relatively quickly, but you're not required to do so in the first sentence. Use your other elements—action and narrative—to acclimate the reader with the details of the scene. This avoids confusion and leaves room for you to continue enhancing the protagonist's characterization.

Exercise: Show, Don't Tell

A good description *shows* rather than tells, what an event or character is like. This is *telling*:

> Leonardo was furious when he arrived at headquarters. He was so pissed he could barely speak.

This is *showing*:

> Leonardo ripped open the door to his office, stomped over to his desk, and threw himself into his seat. He snatched up the phone and hollered at the secretary on the other end.
>
> "Get me the San Diego district office."

Notice that *showing* includes a description of what the character says and does, both of which are filtered through the character's mood and personality. This approach makes the character come alive and provides the reader greater insight into that person.

Exercise: Select one emotion, feeling, or mood. In the example above, we used *furious*, but I encourage you to find your own. Then create a character who *shows* us that adjective through their dialogue, thoughts, behavior, and description. Consider these questions as your guide. Work to make your character believable and realistic. The goal is to use enough detail that the audience can *see* the action.

- Who will your character be?
- What will he or she be doing?
- Where is your character? Home? School? Diner? Are they alone or with friends?
- What happened to make them feel this way?

Using Dialogue to Build Character

As you may recall from previous chapters, the main functions of dialogue are to move the story forward, add tension and conflict, and develop characterization through individuality and interaction. In addition, dialogue humanizes each character and makes them relatable to the reader. Body language, gestures, and sounds are an essential part of dialogue because they accentuate the emotions and subtext behind a character's words. The flare of one's nostrils after a curt response, the gasp of surprise, or the cowed shoulder during an accusation can help amplify the effect of your prose—from magnifying silences to emphasizing the musicality of emotion.

In this chapter, we will focus on dialogue as it refers to character. Dialogue reveals character through the words chosen and the way they are expressed. Therefore, you want to avoid dialogue that sounds scripted. It should match the people you've cultivated, so talk to detectives, lawyers, FBI agents, teachers, plumbers, bakers, or anyone who may understand how your character speaks within their specialized world.

As noted earlier, we should never separate the idea of dialogue from characterization because the two inform each other in a mutually beneficial manner. For example, how a person turns a phrase can let us know if they are angry, surprised, sad, or excited. Someone who doesn't suffer fools lightly may speak in clipped tones—i.e. with short sentences and brash words. While a child who is shy due to an abusive mother, may mumble and reply with a single word. In addition, the way a person speaks—the words used or misused—can give the audience hints about their religion, background, education, and ethnicity.

Remember, when characterization and dialogue are well executed, the reader should be able to develop their own interpretation of the text.

So as a writer, you must train yourself to listen to the characters and allow them to express themselves. You don't want everyone to think and sound like you because that leads to characters acting based on your agenda rather than reacting to the complications of the plot. Make your dialogue true to each person and the situation they're currently facing. Trust that working to better understand your characters' goals, motivations, and conflicts will make writing dialogue easier as well as keep the dialogue consistent with the characterizations that have been developed.

Creating Distinct Characters

Crafting dialogue that's unique to the individual is no simple task. It starts with considering how each person's history and mindset affect their choices. Many writers fail at this first step because they believe that character-specific dialogue begins with picking out catchphrases, slang, regionalisms, verbal tics, et cetera. However, those choices are weak (and cliché) because they are not anchored to the character's inner life.

In other words, don't write your story about a Southern belle who calls everyone *Suga* and loves to bless people's hearts. Write your story about a woman whose recent divorce left her so devasted that she's unable to take anything anyone says at face value. That's someone who's going to garner you great dialogue.

Bottomline: If the dialogue you've created is so superficial that it can work for any of the characters in your story, you haven't done your work properly.

This section is designed to help you avoid that trap.

Build profiles or conduct interviews for all major characters. A profile is where your character talks to you about who they are, what they want, and their purpose within the story. The more time you take to understand your cast—who these people are and what role they play in the manuscript—the more you will have to work with when it is time to create those heartbreaking moments or comedic set pieces that will make your story memorable.

Ask each character the following questions and have them answer in their own voice: What is your main belief about life? What do you aspire to be, have, or do? What do you fear? How do you want other people to see you? How do you see yourself? What aspect of your goals will you talk about freely, and which ones will you hide? All of this will help with your dialogue because you'll start to understand *why* your character has chosen the words or tactics they use. Plus, you'll hear how everyone sounds—their cadence, rhythm, volume, et cetera.

Allow the characters to describe each other. You can also successfully reveal characterization through dialogue by having the characters talk about each other. Now, I'm not referring to the basic elements of direct characterization, where physical attributes and occupations are explicitly described, I'm referring to the gossipy content people share about each other when they have an opinion about that person's attitude or behavior. This speaks volumes about the integrity of the speaker as well as those being discussed. Review this example from *Middlemarch, A Study of Provincial Life* (1876) by George Eliot (aka English author Mary Anne Evans):

> The rural opinion about the new young ladies, even among the cottagers, was generally in favour of Celia, as being so amiable and innocent-looking, while Miss Brooke's large eyes seemed, like her religion, too unusual and striking. Poor Dorothea! Compared with her, the innocent-looking Celia was knowing and worldly-wise.

The narrator offers the town's observations about the two sisters but winds up comparing them in a way that not only helps differentiate the girls but also places an emphasis on the importance of a female's innocence, which is one of the novel's themes.

Let the characters expose themselves. The fastest way to gain insight into a person's character is to show how they behave when no one is watching. For example, show how your character treats hired help (maids, waiters, homeless). Does their status over these people reveal graciousness or cruelty? Or maybe your protagonist is squeamish about touching door handles and constantly checks the locks because he's obsessive-compulsive. Does your heroine cower at the sound of every loud noise because she was bullied as a child? Experiment with the possibilities. Discovering characterization by allowing your characters to expose themselves is much more gratifying for the audience than being saddled with yet another laundry list of useless attributes like eye and hair color.

Tap into each character's feelings. Dialogue should demonstrate the characters' emotions through the way they say or don't say things. This is best achieved through asymmetrical dialogue and subtext, respectively. We'll discuss both in detail later in this book. But the point is that not everyone expresses their emotions the same way. Some people hold things in until they explode. Other people pick fights and become accusatory or disruptive while others might be direct with their confrontations. Some people are spontaneous and speak quickly while others choose their words carefully. To craft a compelling dialogue, you must consider how your characters express themselves when they're highly emotional.

Create Contrasts. Play with the difference between how a character is perceived versus the manner in which they behave. A world class powerlifter who is a sucker for romantic comedies, a seven-year-old who is a Nixon-era savant, or a highly distinguished attorney who is a potty-mouthed misogynist. This dichotomy will create story elements or situations that will influence the dialogue. Imagine crafting a scene where the aforementioned lawyer must litigate a case before a beautiful female judge. What fun you could have with the language as he struggles for politically correct terms.

This can result in dynamic dialogue and subtext that not only differentiates that character's speech patterns from others but also provides humor and insight into that person's personality. Readers are captivated by a character whose personality runs deeper than their initial impression. Plus, there's the added magic of watching the characters in the story misjudge or underestimate that person due to their physical appearance or mental prowess.

Another excellent example of this technique can be found in Isaka Kōtarō's 2010 novel *Maria bītoru* (*Maria Beetle*), translated to English as *Bullet Train* and a decade later turned into similarly titled 2022 feature film starring Brad Pitt. In the book as well as the film, Tangerine and Lemon are a pair of mismatched hitmen tasked with returning the son of a notorious mob boss along with a case full of ransom money. During their journey, it is revealed that Lemon is obsessed with the children's television program *Thomas & Friends* and uses it as a metric to judge character. This infatuation is often played for laughs but also provides the reader insight into Lemon's softer side, making him relatable and likeable despite his occupation.

Spoiler alert: Although the novel and film have drastically different endings, both use Lemon's cuddly character quirk to further drive the plot when Lemon's power of discernment helps him unravel part of the deception that greets them on the train. Bonus points if you, too, can create characterizations that color the dialogue within a scene as well as the overall plot.

Provide unique detail. Quickly bring characters to life by providing an unusual detail about their appearance or behavior. The personality trait or physical attribute you choose should be interesting enough to give the audience a sense of the person's overall behavior and unique enough that it's memorable. While you should certainly work to describe characters throughout a scene, that initial introduction should make a big splash so the reader has an immediate impression. Consider the opening lines of *The Sympathizer* (2016) by Viet Thanh Nguyen:

> I am a spy, a sleeper, a spook, a man of two faces. Perhaps not surprisingly, I am also a man of two minds. I am not some misunderstood mutant from a comic book or a horror movie, although some have treated me as such.

These lines immediately draw the reader forward and cause them to wonder why anyone would refer to themselves in such disparaging terms. We're shocked, but we are also intrigued. And so, we read on, eager to find the answers.

Model someone you know. To distinguish between characters, it may help to latch onto a real person to create a "voice" for your protagonist. Of course, not every real-life aspect of that person will fit into your story, but you can use them as a template for understanding how personal history affects behavior.

Magnify the character's interest. To help individualize your depictions, you may want to focus on the character's hobbies and aspirations. Allow their interest in law enforcement or an ideology like Buddhism to act as the lens through which they see the world. This would naturally color how they speak and what they'd notice about the environment. For example, someone who has spent several years in the military may have a very rigid definition of loyalty or right versus wrong. Perhaps, she would speak in short clipped sentences and say "affirmative" rather than "yup." In other words, her perspective and outlook can speak to her motive and actions.

Utilize diction. Once you've found the character's inner life, word choice can become a powerful way to develop a character's voice and enhance characterization. Just think about the different ways people say hello:

- Howdy.
- Hi.
- Yo!
- Hiya!
- Hey!
- What's up?
- 'Sup?

Each one speaks volumes about the type of person you're going to encounter in terms of education, attitude, et cetera. Consider the characters of Eugene and Abraham from the television series *The Walking Dead*. Both characters speak in an odd manner that's nearly identical except that Eugene's motivation for word choice and cadence is to demonstrate his intelligence while Abraham uses language to dominate and/or ridicule in the most macho manner possible.

EUGENE:

I'm serious as coronary thrombosis.

ABRAHAM:

When are you going to spill the pintos?

With these examples in mind, here are some basic verbal markers you can use to individualize characters:

- **Contractions** – shortening a word or word group by removing a sound, letter, or syllable; (y'all, we'll, they'd)
- **Elisions** – a speech form that drops the final or initial sound; (doin', goin', 'cuz)
- **Interjections** – a sudden exclamation that conveys emotion; this category also includes foul language, which is discussed in a separate section; (Doc Brown: "Great Scott!" or Annie: "Leaping Lizards!")
- **Slang** – informal diction often dictated by popular culture; avoid material that will date your work; (*cringe, on fleek, straight fire, that slaps*)
- **Idioms** – an expression that's distinctive to specific language or culture; the meaning of these phrases often cannot be derived from the literal meaning of the words; try to create your own to avoid cliché; (e.g. I need another credit card like I need *a hole in the head.*)
- **Idiolects** – slightly peculiar phrases distinctive to a specific person; (e.g. Trey from *Sex and the City* uses "All righty" when the rest of the world would say, "No problem.")

It may be helpful to keep a style sheet to track how characters speak and what expressions they typically use. This will help maintain consistency throughout the book. A style sheet is simply a document that lists the grammar and usage choices you made while writing the manuscript.

Experiment with how the characters use language. Is your hero a fast talker, or is he marble-mouthed with an accent? Does your heroine talk over people and use authoritative phrases, or does she speak softly because of her limited vocabulary? Maybe you have a character who avoids contractions because they don't ever feel like they are being heard so to state everything outright adds emphasis to their declarations: "*Do not* touch me ever again!" Work to give your characters distinct speech patterns. Things that may assist you with those decisions include age, social status, culture, education, temperament, personal history, and the character's opinion about the overall story question.

Utilize the five senses. Determine which senses your characters prefer and use them as a way to flesh out behavior. Visual characters may be more attuned to expressing ideas in terms of imagery, color, and spectacle while aural characters may be loquacious, lyrical, and full of onomatopoeia. Touchy-feely folks may rely more on gesture and proximity than the words themselves. And of course, those who focus on smell or taste, might be more reliant on their head or gut instincts than the average person.

Experiment with how the character sounds. People rarely use the same tone for every conversation. On a job interview, they may be quieter and more formal than a conversation with a friend for whom they may be rambunctious and loud. So in addition to choosing the right words, think about how that language sounds. Is it poetic, bordering on lyrical? Is it brash and somewhat baritone? Study these additional characteristics and determine how you can use them to distinguish your protagonist's voice from the crowd:

- Tone (attitude)
- Diction (word choice)
- Classification (bass to soprano)
- Pitch, intensity, and timbre (tonal quality)
- Rhythm (lyrical, clipped, languid, et cetera)
- Foul language (yes or no)

Here are some final reminders for making your characters and their dialogue memorable:

- Identify each character's internal needs, wants, goals, and wounds (their psychological sticking point).

- Consider your characters' belief systems. What drives them?
- Avoid clichés. Strive to develop unusual personality traits that are grounded in their belief systems.
- Look for opportunities to create contrasting personality traits within the individual and the overall cast. This will make it easier to devise internal and external conflict.
- Construct impactful introductions for each character.
- Be careful about using too many idiolects at one time and repeating them too frequently. This can quickly become obnoxious to the audience. Remember, readers often pay more attention to dialogue than the narrative, so any idiosyncrasies buried within speech are magnified. Always be subtle about adding any character oddities. Less is more.

Exercise: Creating Distinct Characters

Exercise: Select a character who plays a crucial role in your manuscript, and consider how you plan to introduce them. What are the strongest ways to show their personality? What do they believe is most important in life, and how does that belief dictate the way they interact with the world? How can you make that outlook or behavior humorous? Challenge yourself to create the most impactful introduction possible.

Goals and Motivation

When writing dialogue, it is best to begin with understanding what you'd like the dialogue to do—deepen character, advance the plot, or convey information. The next step is to identify the emotional context of the scene. What headspace do we find our characters occupying, and what's the conflict at hand? Are they secretly in love with each other and afraid to show it? Are they recovering from a harrowing near-death situation? Is one person jealous of the other? The answer will affect how the scene unfolds. Remember, people don't talk aimlessly in fiction. There must be a purpose or a conflict that the parties involved are attempting to navigate.

The writer's job is to inform the reader, in the most seamless manner possible, what each character wants (goal), why they want it (motive), and their plan for getting it (tactics)—even if the characters aren't consciously aware of these things. These goals and motivations can be internal or external, but they are always what drive the character to act throughout the story. Therefore, you cannot build a scene without first identifying these elements:

- What does each character want to happen? (Goal)
- What is at stake for each character in the scene? What do they stand to gain or lose in pursuit of their goal? (Motivation)
- What will it cost each character to get what she wants? (Conflict)

Once goals and motivations have been established, you can easily demonstrate them to the audience by what the characters say (dialogue) and how they behave (action). These two tools are especially useful for those people whose thoughts we aren't privy to during the course of the scene. As you write, don't create polite scenes that imitate real life. Instead, create contrasts between characters so not only do they want opposing things, but they also have different approaches to pursuing those desires. This becomes the fuel for conflict, which we will discuss in the next section.

In closing, once readers are clear about what each character wants, they start to anticipate the potential for things to go wrong. Anticipation breeds tension and builds suspense—the two elements that keep readers glued to the page.

Exercise: Goals and Motivation

Exercise: Select a scene from your manuscript, and determine the goal and motivation for each character in the scene. Write a passage of dialogue based on your decisions. Make note of the scene's new tone, pacing, conflict, and tension. Now, go back and change everyone's goals and motivations to see how that will affect your dialogue. What new tactics did your characters use to get what they want? Has the pace changed? Is the tension still high?

Conflict, Tension, and Suspense

A conflict is a problem or predicament or opposing force or obstacle that keeps a character from getting what they want. Many writers believe that in addition to the story's overarching conflict, there should also be conflict in every line of dialogue. If the idea of constant conflict has you hyperventilating, enhance your calm.

Conflict isn't about constant fist fights. It's about taking the goals, motives, tactics of one character and pitting them against a character with an opposing agenda. For stories whose main thrust isn't *character v. character* but rather *character v. nature* or *character v. themself*, then the conflict would take the form of an obstacle such as a hurricane or self-doubt. Be advised that not every antagonist or obstacle needs to be literal life or death, but it should *feel* like it to the protagonist. It's his *belief* about the situation that's paramount. That's why movies like *Ferris Bueller's Day Off* (1986) and *Armageddon* (1998) both work despite the differing magnitudes in the obstacles and stakes.

In other words, conflict is measured by what's important to the viewpoint character. So make sure you know your characters well enough to anticipate how they will react when presented with a challenge. This will be the crux of your dialogue and will determine which direction your plot will take.

In either case—antagonist or obstacle—each scene would end with some change having occurred as a result of the conflict. A change that shifts the outlook or agenda of the viewpoint character for that scene. This could be as small as a strategy shift or as large as a modification of their belief system. In essence, conflict is a vital part of storytelling because it helps to illustrate the difference in personality between your characters, identifies their values, and propels them forward through the plot.

On the other hand, if nothing changes, you need to reevaluate your work. Every scene should turn the story. Stagnate characters create stagnate dialogue—both of which alienate your audience. Remember, the reader wants to play an active role in your story, and conflict is one of the ways we bring the reader into the fold. By showing the audience what this character stands to gain or lose as they go up against each new challenge, they start to feel for him, worry for him, anticipate how he may eventually overcome—and it's that audience investment that keeps them riveted to the page.

You will find that your best dialogue comes when the scene's two opposing forces are at their greatest odds. That's because your scene will be riding at its highest tension as both characters fight for or defend the respective strategies.

Conflict in dialogue is simple when the conflict is external. But how do we develop dialogue for conflict that's internal? While direct thoughts help to active an inner struggle, there should be a point when that internal conflict is externalized so the audience can experience the character taking direct action toward their goal. What is the character consciously hiding from himself or the audience? What is the character hiding from themselves that they haven't yet realized? What is the character not yet aware of that may be driving them subconsciously? Remember, deception and secrecy feed conflict. And of course, the more powerful the conflict, the easier it is to captivate the reader.

Tension

Every dialogue exchange must contain conflict and tension.

Tension is the immediate feeling of discomfort that occurs when a dreaded or anticipated action or event comes to fruition.

Be advised that tension isn't always a physical confrontation. This could simply be a problem, a difference in opinion or interpretation, contrary preferences, thwarted effort, or when the viewpoint character realizes the situation may not be exactly what it seems. Conflict and tension can even emerge from benign situations such as a character's reluctance. Think about the last time your friend asked to borrow a couple bucks, but you didn't think they deserved it or you really couldn't afford to give it. That situation isn't necessary grounds for a fight, but I bet it's one that could be rife with tension due to the opposing agendas of lending money versus keeping money.

In other words, there should be a lot more occurring during the exchange than what's being said on the surface. We also don't want our characters having a pleasant conversation even if they are allies. When every exchange is sweet, the dialogue doesn't have the power to propel the story forward. Tense dialogue, whether an argument or a seemingly innocent white lie, adds intensity and unpredictability to the scene.

Again, I can't stress this enough: You must have some conflict and tension in every scene, or you risk losing the audience. If your scene has no conflict, you can probably put that information into a summary for the narrative elements of the chapter. To help build conflict that breeds tension, identify the obstacle for each scene. For example, if two characters are discussing an urgent issue, an interruption from another character at a high point of contention adds a momentary obstacle, creating a slice of tension.

Here are four additional ways to add tension to dialogue:

Write tight. When you keep sentences short, the scene maintains a brisk pace, which is ideal for conflict. Plus, the snappiness of the quick back and forth creates friction. Similarly, use tone (attitude) to increase the tension by make the language pointed and crisp. This can take the form of snarky questions, sarcastic responses, and stern commands—all of which tend to have a gruffer edge.

Use asymmetrical dialogue. We will cover this concept more closely in its own chapter, but it is basically the remedy to on-the-nose dialogue. Rather than have your characters answer each other directly, allow them to contradict each other, cut each other off, answer a question with a question, change topics, et cetera. The dialogue should still move forward, it's just that the characters are leading with their emotions rather than their rational mind. So, they are more focused on their respective agendas than having a straightforward conversation. Plus, the simple fact that there's a push and pull between the two characters about how to handle the issue is a major nod to tension.

Incorporate subtext and silence. Often, the best tension comes from what the characters fail to say to each other—what they hide about themselves for fear of being judged or what they hold back for fear of ruining the relationship. The reader takes pleasure in reading between the lines, knowing there is more to the story.

Torture your characters. You want to make things as bad as possible for your characters. Don't be afraid to have them encounter their worst fears. After all, good fiction is about the struggle of overcoming obstacles. The reader wants to see how the character resolves their problems. Will the protagonist remain on the straight and narrow or resort to something more sinister that the reader can experience vicariously through them?

End the scene with an intriguing line. Use the final line to create the kind of tension that will compel the audience to keep reading. The key is to avoid ending the scene with statements that resolve everything in a perfectly tidy manner. Leave things open-ended like a mini-cliffhanger. If there's a knock on the door, end the scene with the reaction in the room, not entrance of the intruder. Or conversely, perhaps a character makes a shocking statement, rather than have the room respond, let the words linger. Give them room to breathe. This will give the reader a moment to ponder the significance and assume the worst.

Suspense

Suspense is the audience's emotional interest in the outcome of the story. That interest may amount to fear, hope, or uncertainty. Audiences love suspense because they like to see how characters deal with adversity. We imagine ourselves in the same situation and try to predict the outcome for the protagonist. In essence, suspense allows the reader to face their fears in a controlled environment, which is exhilarating—dare I say, thrilling.

DIFFERENCE BETWEEN TENSION AND SUSPENSE

In 2022, a national cable company ran a very effective series of ads about their services for the hearing impaired. In one commercial, a television viewer stops the action of her favorite show to ask the characters to speak louder. This prompts them to hold up signs that eventually turn into closed captioning. But as the characters create their signs, a brief argument ensues over the description of the music as "tense" or "suspenseful," prompting one character to ask: "Aren't they the same thing?"

Not quite. We tend to conflate the terms because their narrative purposes are connected and it could be argued that one is a byproduct of the other. However, when we look at their definitions, there is a slight distinction. Tension is the *physical* manifestation in the present brought on by conflict while suspense is the psychological *feeling* manifested by posing a dilemma and delaying the answer. In other words, the tension is found in the moment of the act, and suspense is found in the anticipation of the act or the outcome.

Does this mean you need to drastically alter how you speak about these terms? Maybe, maybe not. I fully admit I sometimes use them as synonyms in this book. However, it is important that you are aware of the difference in execution because that knowledge may help you craft better dialogue.

BUILDING SUSPENSE

Suspense builds when the audience has empathy for the characters. The reader fears the worse and hopes for the best—all while being unsure, or at least apprehensive, about what's actually going to happen. Suspense can be an unresolved high-stakes situation or a delayed resolution, but it is something that creates enough uncertainty that the audience is either dying to know what happens next or they *think* they know what happens next. Obviously, smart authors subvert those predictions or expectations with an unanticipated solution that falls somewhere between the readers' hopes and fears. Never give the reader what they expect. If you do that, what's the point of them reading your book? Give them a reason to keep turning pages by developing a fresh approach.

A popular way to create suspense is through dramatic irony, which is when your audience knows more than your characters. The suspense grows as we wonder if and when the protagonist will discover what we already know. Consider *Die Hard* (1988) when John McClane meets Hans Gruber near the roof of the Nakatomi building and gives him a gun. We squeal and yell at the screen because we know Gruber is the bad guy, and we think our hero has just written his own death sentence.

Even though the scenario doesn't transpire exactly how we anticipate (turns out, McClane gives Gruber an unloaded gun), the technique succeeds in developing a sympathetic connection between the audience and the protagonist—*will he or won't he get out of the impending predicament*—while reinforcing the readers' desire to see what happens next.

Another useful way to add suspense is to give each character a guilty secret or dark past that they are working hard to keep hidden. This can be used to make your characters behave in mysterious ways that cause conflict and tension. These secrets might develop and unfold over the course of the story, or they can be presented from the start as something the audience and protagonist knows but the rest of the cast doesn't. The suspense comes from the audience's fear—*will she or won't she be exposed*. This approach can work in any genre, but it is especially good for humor or romance where characters are often trying to avoid being viewed as liars or frauds. Consider films like *Maid in Manhattan* (2005) or *Sister Act* (1992).

Suspense can also be created when characters talk about the prowess of a character who has not yet appeared. The suspense comes from the anticipation of how that person's skill can hurt the hero or alter the story's path away from the desired ending. This approach can be especially powerful when applied to a character who is feared or ruthless in some manner like Marcellus Wallce in *Pulp Fiction* (1994).

How does this translate to dialogue? The words your characters use are the best way to inform or misinform the reader about what's happening. A character's deception or another's misinterpretation of events put the audience in a position where they *think* they know what's happening, but there is so much more going on under the surface. That's why it is important that you deliver information slowly. Avoid giving everything away at once. But be careful, some people will read this and think I am saying you should keep things vague and not give the audience any information at all. Do not fall for that interpretation.

Writing suspenseful dialogue is about giving the audience as much information as they need to understand what's at stake or to recognize the proximity of danger or to calculate the improbability of escape. Think about it. Readers can't enjoy the story if they're left in the dark for most of it. As noted at the top of the chapter, the joy of suspense comes from recognizing that bad things are on the horizon. It comes from fearing the worst while hoping for the best.

By learning about the situation, we share in the character's anxiety and we begin to feel for them, which keeps us invested in the action. So to create this delicate web of suspense with your dialogue, it may help to ask yourself this: Once I've decided what the audience needs to know to understand this scene, what tiny part of each character's strategy should I conceal to put the potential outcome into question?

Gestures & Body Language

Gestures are a character-specific movement that can enhance the imagery or action of a scene. But because every element of a story must serve a purpose, a truly strong gesture should also do the following:

- Provide a visual for the reader
- Connect the speaker to the spoken word and setting
- Mirror emotions
- Reinforce the dialogue's meaning
- Show how language is spoken and how words are received

As you develop your narrative, think about the gestures, mannerisms, and body language your characters will use to interact with each other. These actions should reflect each character's personality and go beyond the smiles, nods, frowns, shrugs, and smirks that run rampant in almost every manuscript. Remember, figurative language like similes, metaphors, and personification can aid you in creating gestures that favor feeling over filler and show rather than tell. Strive to create useful gestures that underscore the dialogue without undermining its power.

Use your gestures to activate the dialogue by...

- **Clarifying character:** He slammed his fist into the wall. "Screw you."
- **Showing the difference between inward feeling and outward speech:** She clenched her jaw and sighed. "Yeah, sure, I'll marry you."
- **Establishing an emotion or mood:** "And your little dog too." The wicked witch cracked a wide smile that exposed a sharp set of yellowing teeth.
- **Creating a pause between dialogue passages:** "Quiet!" Her

voice echoed off the cave walls and dissipated into stillness.
- **Highlighting a crucial moment:** "I love you t—" I clamped a hand over my mouth already wishing I could take the words back.
- **Heighten tension:** He pressed the tip of the knife against the delicate flesh behind her ear.

You can also allow action and gestures to replace lines of dialogue whenever appropriate. This gives the audience an opportunity to interact with the text and draw their own conclusions about what the character may be thinking and feeling. Trust that body language can communicate your characters' emotions just as powerfully as the spoken word. Besides, the more movement you can add to your characters' verbalizations, the easier it will be for your reader to identify each speaker.

In addition, try using the physical aspects of a space to help create mannerisms that reveal information about your character. Look for objects that can act as props for your players. Use them to command attention, create a pause, or define a silence. These objects can be almost anything a person uses in their daily lives—a hair brush, hand grenade, or harp. Animals can sometimes become props as well. Just avoid having your character speak aloud to the pet for long stretches.

Objects, like body language, can help reveal a character's mood through the gestures associated with use of the prop. For instance, a person who walks into his apartment and throws his briefcase against the wall demonstrates his frustrations about work. Similarly, physical actions—like twirling hair, biting nails, or cracking knuckles—can speak to mental state, so allow your characters to use parts of their anatomy or clothing as an additional way to interact with the environment.

But as with everything, use this technique in moderation and make sure that you're selecting objects that say something specific about the characters. We always want our use of added objects to advance the scene or tie into some larger element of the plot.

And lastly, don't be afraid to use sensory elements as a way to enhance your gestures. First, determine which senses your characters prefer and use them as a way to flesh out behavior. Visual characters may be more attuned to expressing ideas in terms of imagery, color, and spectacle while aural characters may be loquacious, lyrical, and full of onomatopoeia. Just be mindful that you're showing, not telling. For example, words like *he noticed, he felt, he heard, he smelled, he tasted* put distance between the reader and the character. Stay inside the character's head and describe the emotion from within.

>Weak: Jacob noticed everyone was staring at him.

>Strong: Jacob's skin turned red with embarrassment.

>Weak: She felt the cold water against her skin.

>Strong: An icy stream of water cascaded down her neck.

Similarly, use physical touch to show relationships. Hugs and kisses show love, handshakes indicate respect, a pat on the back implies encouragement, et cetera. Avoid adding a gesture or an action beat "just to fill space" or "just because there hasn't been any movement in a while" or "just because it would be cool." Your character's movements should have a purpose that clarifies the setting or conflict.

A WORD ON FACIAL EXPRESSIONS

Editors always ask writers to avoid describing facial expressions as a "dark look" because that doesn't show or tell the audience what that person is doing with their face. This is kind of like a film's cinematographer attempting to use a wide shot to convey the protagonist's internal agony. The lack of focus on the character's face would make it difficult for the viewer to understand their turmoil. Since films aren't able to include the internal work we rely upon as authors, the camera zooms in tight for the closeup. We see the beads of sweat on the brow, the trembling lip, and the flared nostrils that speaks to the character's emotions.

Although the idea of a tight shot is a cinematic element, we novelist still want to show or describe our characters' faces in strong and innovative ways. To do this, we can couple the characters' thoughts with a specific facial expression, action, or emotion that hints at subtext. Don't be afraid to use them all in combination. Consider this example from *The Hunger Games* (2008) by Suzanne Collins.

> As I enter the dining car, Effie Trinket brushes by me with a cup of black coffee. She's muttering obscenities under her breath. Haymitch, his face puffy and red from the previous day's indulgences, is chuckling. Peeta holds a roll and looks somewhat embarrassed.

Notice how this example has the narrator alighting briefly on the faces of each character like a film camera, yet facial expressions weren't the sole means of description. The passage also relies on action and emotion to set the scene and create tension. This is crucial if you want to get in your editor's good graces.

When revising your manuscript, ensure that all the facial expression, gestures, body language, habits, and mannerisms add value to the story by deepening characterization. Also, be clear about why you selected one gesture over another and avoid any mannerisms that read like filler or caricature.

Exercise: Gestures & Body Language

Exercise #1: Brainstorm a list of locations that may be helpful to your writing. Find time to visit each of those places and create a list of gestures you use when occupying that space. What actions surface when you're standing in line at the grocery store? How do you react when you enter a dark movie theater? What's your response when a door slams in a public restroom? Even though these reactions, gestures, and actions are specific to you, rather than your characters, it will give you some idea of how far you can take tings the next time you write a scene in one of those locations.

Exercise #2: Select one or two objects and decide how to incorporate them into a scene. Draft dialogue that references the items. If you're unsure what to choose, look around you. Common household items like a remote control, a coffee mug, scissors, or a couch pillow can aid in storytelling and spark compelling subtext.

Subtext

Subtext is the meaning beneath the dialogue. This includes the beliefs or ideas a character may feel or want to divulge but can't because of personal circumstances, self-censorship, or an inability to articulate one's emotions. This juxtaposition between what is said versus what is meant creates tension that colors each interaction; therefore subtext, like dialogue, can be used to fuel conflict, reveal character, and advance the plot.

HOW DO YOU CREATE SUBTEXT?

The fastest way to create subtext is to ensure your characters are engaged in conflict and replace all your on-the-nose dialogue with a more nuanced layer.

But to get to the point, you'll first need to look for words or phrases where a character states outright how they feel or what they want. This is the exact opposite of what you want. While having those things on the surface may seem like the most direct way to finish your scene, it often manifests as telling and removes the conflict and tension from your story.

So in order to turn things toward subtext, you must create a reason why your character is hesitant or unwilling to speak the truth about that surface information. Remember, subtext is about the hidden meaning, so what would cause them to be more guarded moving forward? Do they stand to lose something? Will they be prone to ridicule? Are they fearful their feelings won't be appreciated or reciprocated?

Once you have your motivation, you can start to see how the character might conceal certain feelings behind their modified behavior, attitude, or word choice. Those guarded behaviors act as huge sign post for the audience because now you're showing them how this person's inability to show their true feelings affects them and fuels their interactions, which ultimately drives the story. Remember, we as writers always want to show rather than tell.

Develop your characters well enough that you would naturally understand their emotional depths and how they play into the story's stakes. Figure out how they will react to the different obstacles they encounter—both based on how they are feeling in the moment as well as feelings they may need to suppress in order to get the job done.

When it comes to crafting subtext, you want to anchor your protagonist's dialogue to an emotional state without overtly stating or putting a definitive label on that emotion. This works both in fiction and in real life. Think about it. If we're feeling down, we tend to lash out. If we're nervous or excited, we may become standoffish.

As noted in *GMC: Goal, Motivation, and Conflict*, the legendary writer's manual by Debra Dixon, we should develop our characters so they act and speak in a manner that aligns with their goals for the scene. Note that when a character wants something, there should always be something or someone else to oppose that desire. This means that your character will need several approaches or modes of attack in order to succeed. As you develop those different tactics for your character, you will begin to notice that many of them involve elements like agreeing, lying, flattering, cheating, arguing, et cetera. That list doesn't include every approach, but based on those entries, we can see where subtext may develop since they all conceal the truth of what your hero may want.

As stated earlier, a character should rarely make a straightforward declaration because it causes the scene to grind to a halt due to predictable behavior and lack of tension. Do the math. A direct query usually amounts to direct reply, which ends the conflict and does nothing to move your scene forward.

HOW TO CRAFT KILLER DIALOGUE

Consider this exchange from *Devil in a Blue Dress* (1990) by Walter Mosley. In this passage, subtext is created because Easy Rawlins is not giving direct replies. In fact, his thoughts run counter to his words, which creates a fair amount of tension. Indeed, that's quite a feat considering the scene is essentially an introduction between strangers.

> "Com'on over here, Easy. This here's somebody I want ya t'meet."
>
> I could feel those pale eyes on me.
>
> "This here's a ole friend'a mines, Easy. Mr. Albright."
>
> "You can call me DeWitt, Easy," the white man said. His grip was strong but slithery, like a snake coiling around my hand.
>
> "Hello," I said.
>
> "Yeah, Easy," Joppy went on, bowing and grinning. "Mr. Albright and me go way back. You know he prob'ly my oldest friend from L.A. Yeah, we got ways back."
>
> "That's right," Albright smiled. "It must've been 1935 when I met Jop. What is it now? Must be thirteen years. That was back before the war, before every farmer, and his brother's wife, wanted to come to L.A."
>
> Joppy guffawed at the joke; I smiled politely. I was wondering what kind of business Joppy had with that man and, along with that, I wondered what kind of business that man could have with me.
>
> "Where you from, Easy?" Mr. Albright asked.
>
> "Houston."

As note earlier, subtext is often about a character suppressing their emotions or opinions. In this instance, we have Easy Rawlings, the protagonist of the story, thinking that DeWitt is a snake, but does he say that? No way. In fact, he doesn't say much. Just two words, but those responses speak volumes. The subtext is clear: Easy wants nothing to do with this untrustworthy man.

People don't always say what they mean, but subtext is a way to demonstrate those moments to the reader. If you're receiving feedback that your dialogue is predictable, your work is probably lacking subtext. Luckily, the remedy is simple: Rather than always having your characters take the direct approach, have them interact with a hidden agenda and let their body language, mannerisms, and thoughts hint at the truth.

All good dialogue should have subtext, which is the push and pull between what a character says and what a character means. Consider subtext, as a concept, the epitome of *show, don't tell* where we leave things open for the audience's interpretation.

As you continue to incorporate more subtext into your work, consider the following strategies to assist you:

- Incorporate body language that runs contrary to the dialogue.
- Place focus on objects in the setting that have symbolic significance or multiple meanings.
- Allow the conversation to skirt around an unspoken topic.
- Use the environment to conjure references to past experiences or events.
- Focus on an aspect of the characters' mutual history that you can convey in another form such as metaphor, symbolism, or theme.

Exercise: Subtext

Exercise: Consider a recent life event where a message lurked beneath the dialogue. Perhaps your boss discussed a poor performing coworker during your last private meeting, but you believe it was a passive-aggressive inference to your own performance. Whatever the scenario, create a solo scene that showcases subtext. Focus on how the elements of that situation that can be communicated through body language, voice, emotion, intention, and interpretation.

Silence in Dialogue

A silent response can be just as powerful as a spoken one. Silence can indicate a plethora of things—agreement, disgust, denial, or shock—depending on the situation. Use facial expressions or gestures to fill the silence and shape that nonverbal response so that it speaks volumes. In other words, rather than state that there's a silence, replace it with an action beat.

Weak: He stared at her, but didn't say anything.

Strong: He stared at her.

Strong: He stared at her until she walked away.

If he's staring, that's enough. The act alone implies silence. That's why the second example is better. The third example also works because now we have a time period for the stare and some additional action for the scene. Notice how the stronger examples don't overplay the silence by adding the adverb *silently*. The implication through action is enough.

"Admit it. You never wanted to get married."

John sunk down onto the sofa.

"Did you ever love me?"

He cradled his head in his hands.

"Then why go through with it?"

Silence is a statement. Silence is a response. Silence is a trigger for action. When a character refuses to respond, the reader instantly knows something is not as it should be. The narrative doesn't need to state

Ralph wasn't ready to discuss his feelings because some situations are universal. That's why silence is sometimes more powerful than words—it heightens the tension the reader feels and pushes the subtext to the forefront.

So don't be afraid to add silence to your dialogue. After all, people rarely speak ad nauseum. Plus, it is a great way to break up blocks of text or regulate the pace of a scene that would otherwise be too brisk. But be mindful that creating silence is often the act of pulling back, rather than adding on. Restraint is key, so it helps to declutter the scene by putting the narrative focus on the two people who are at odds. Think of it zooming into closeup on your characters.

And most importantly, make sure all of your silences serve a purpose and speak to the character's inner life. Nothing is worse than an author who uses silence as filler or because they've given up on the exchange. If that's the case, your scene probably lacks conflict and/or does not connect with the larger story question.

Exercise: Silence in Dialogue

Exercise #1: If this approach to incorporating silence is new to you, brainstorm several situations where things going quiet could speak volumes about the people in the scene or a potential conflict—e.g. a blind date, a couple celebrating their 50th anniversary, Thanksgiving with that one racist uncle, et cetera.

Exercise #2: Write a short scene where two characters argue, but structure the exchange so that only one of them has direct dialogue. Allow the other character to narrate the scene. Weave together action, thought, description, narrative, and backstory to create the story. Once you're finished, examine how you created silences for your viewpoint character. What meaning did they hold? How did they propel the argument? How effective were they?

The Power of the Pause

Your approach to the pause should mirror the one used for silences. We want to illustrate breaks in the conversation through gestures and action. The narrative does need to say, *Keisha waited a beat before responding.* Consider these examples:

Weak: "John," she paused, "could I borrow your car tonight?"

Strong: "John?" She pressed her breasts against his shoulder as she leaned into his ear. "Could I borrow your car tonight?"

The second one is great because we see the tactic she uses to get what she wants. As a result, we understand the motivation for how John might respond. Here are a few more that contain common errors:

Weak: "Wait." Tanisha paused and blinked back tears. "You don't love me anymore?"

Strong: "Wait." Tanisha blinked back tears. "You don't love me anymore?"

Weak: "No deal." Hiro paused to lick his lips and gather his thoughts. "But I wouldn't mind a trade."

Strong: "No deal." Hiro licked lips as if lost in thought. "But I wouldn't mind a trade."

If you want to keep it simple, indicate the pause with an ellipsis rather than including the dialogue tag.

Weak: "I don't know what I want for dinner." She paused. "Pizza? Maybe a calzone?"

Strong: "I don't know what I want for dinner . . . pizza? Maybe a calzone?"

Strong: "I don't know what I want for dinner." She twirled a strand of hair around her index finger. "Pizza? Maybe a calzone?"

Pauses, unlike silences, don't need to be quiet. The action beats we use can contain growls, groans, catcalls, and even music. Anything that denotes a passage of time works. For example, you can use descriptions or thoughts to fill a pause because those observations indicate that the characters have momentarily stopped what they're saying to change focus. This might also be where you unpack their personal opinions about the exchange.

"Look, man, the plan is foolproof. All you have to do is keep watch outside the teacher's lounge."

"I don't know . . ." Dennis bit at the large hang nail on his thumb, and let the wall clock tick along to the guitar riff echoing in his head. What's the worst that could happen? A week's expulsion? That's five extra days to finish his demo. "Sure, I'm down."

And of course, just like silence, our pauses should serve a purpose—i.e. clarifying actions or aiding characterization. Avoid using pauses as filler. In such instances, you run the risk of overdoing things and diluting their effectiveness.

The smartest way to utilize a pause is to have it underscore an important event, decision, or revelation. A pause that occurs right before the executioner's axe falls, or in the moments preceding a long-awaited confession, creates curiosity and anxiety in the audience. In other words, select a pivotal point of change and use the pause to create tension. Force the reader to wonder, *what's going to happen next* and *what will be the fallout*?

In addition, there are certain elements of a story that you shouldn't rush through such as the exposure of a secret, the discovery of a deception, or the formulation of a plan—i.e. things that would occur at the climax of a scene. Slow the dialogue down in those spots or create a pause. You can do this by downshifting the pause to silence. This will help the audience slow down, look around, and experience the gravity of the moment.

Humor

It's natural to want to laugh. It's fun, easy to do, and part of what makes us feel good.

To be funny, you must be a student of human nature and popular culture. Rather than stressing yourself out trying to make up things from scratch, look to what's familiar. Find what's currently circulating in the zeitgeist and create universal connections so that the story you're telling and the humor you're infusing it with can touch a larger audience. Audiences instinctively know when you're trying too hard to be clever or when the observations you make are disingenuous. Humor must come from the heart. Humor is truth. It's being brutally honest about those things that bring us joy and pain.

Humor is also a great way to disarm people and soften the approach to a message they might not otherwise accept. Comedy can create a unifying common ground between disparate camps. It is a great way to examine the world around you, to figure out how the world works, and to develop a perspective on life. Laughter connects the audience to your work with a visceral involuntary response—it gets them on your side.

However, having rapport with someone and developing humor in a real-life conversation is different from establishing humor between two characters in a story. On the page, you need to understand your characters' points of view.

IDENTIFY THE COMIC VOICE

Determine your characters' comedic voice by deciding from what perspective, or lens, they want to tell their stories. Is it a cultural lens? Did they grow up in a unique household? Are they a jaded pessimist who can only see the dark side of a situation? Do they approach everything from an academic viewpoint so each humorous observation has a moral lesson that viewers are meant to ponder long after the story ends? Figure out what aspects of their background, interests, and personality will help determine their comedic voice. You will be surprised how clarifying this one element will make it easier to write.

Also, read widely both inside and outside your genre because you never know what disparate piece of information will help you make connections when you're trying to develop humor.

Partner with the smartest person you know and discuss comedy. If the two of you are having a tough time finding your funny bones, read the work of authors known for their comedy. Some of my favorite include Deborah Coonts, Gretchen Archer, Andrew Shaffer, Donna Andrews, Kate Carlisle, and Janet Evanovich. However, I encourage you to create a list of artists specific to your goals and tastes. Examine what aspects of storytelling the writers use to craft the laugh. An exaggerated premise? Embarrassing conflicts? Farce? Word choice? Traditional jokes with puns and punchlines?

Another easy way to add humor to your writing, if you're new to the genre, is to quote funny people. Borrow sayings from your funny friends or recycle lines overhead in passing on the street. Avoid copyrighted material unless doing a review and providing the original author full credit. You can also use hyperbole, which is a heightened exaggeration of events. We do this every day when telling our friends about a tense or exciting situation. This practice of stretching a scenario to its most ridiculous extremes will translate well to your humor writing.

Also, keep in mind that certain words are inherently funny. Odd numbers are funnier than even numbers. Words associated with the "k" or "c" sounds are considered hilarious like "kerchief" (instead of scarf) or "cannonball" (rather than dive). Onomatopoeia words, or words that evoke the sound they define. "Kerplunk" or "splat." Other words become funny based on the image created. Either way, putting the funny word at the end of the sentence helps.

You may also want to develop a list of humorous topics to include in your book. Do some research, if necessary, to find out if there are certain tropes about comedy in your genre. When you're talking to people, notice the types of things they find funny, especially if they begin to riff on those things. That's a huge indicator that the situation might be ripe for a scene or story.

Remember, if you have a great premise and great characters, finding a way to make it funny should be easy.

GIVE THEM SOMETHING UNEXPECTED

You always want to be one step ahead of the audience in comedy. Allowing them to figure out the punchline before it's delivered ruins the joke's effectiveness, so work to subvert expectations surrounding the humor in a scene. Change the tempo of your jokes and be uneven in your delivery so the audience is off-balance and they have to pay extra attention to what you're doing to build the punchline.

Zig when the audience zags. Take the surface meaning for a joke or punchline and transform it into something the audience isn't expecting. Work toward original ideas. While you want to stick with your instinct, try to avoid the first idea that pops into your head because it is likely cliché. The best way to be original is to get specific. Clear choices make for richer comedy.

The joke's setup creates tension by navigating the reader's attention in a specific direction thus setting up an expectation. There may be varying levels of banter and worldbuilding in the middle to sustain that tension, but ultimately the arc of the joke must come to an end to be successful. That ending place is the punchline where expectations have been subverted and supplanted by something unexpected (and hopefully better than anticipated) and the tension will be released.

Although the finished joke may feel unpredictable to the audience, the writer must be clear on the structure. Be precise because the framework you create will guide the audience's attention in the direction you want them to go. Consider this example from *The Absolutely True Diary of a Part-Time Indian* (2007) by Sherman Alexie:

> "I used to think the world was broken down by tribes," I said. "By Black and White. By Indian and White. But I know this isn't true. The world is only broken into two tribes: the people who are assholes and the people who are not."

This dialogue exhibits the three parts of a joke: the setup, the reversal, and the punchline. I'm not saying all of your characters should walk around telling jokes—after all, your dialogue should serve the plot; however, this is a great technique to have in your toolbox to create moments of levity when needed. Again, every story should have a little bit of humor because humor recognizes the human condition. Just don't use anyone's physical appearance as the source of comedy. The best kind of joke is one that you don't see coming; it starts early and pays off much later.

Beginning, Middle, End ⇒ Setup, Reversal, Punchline.

If you're not able to create a compelling narrative, you won't be able to craft good comedy.

Use your opening line to set the tone. Is the comedy you're delivering going to be esoteric? Slapstick? Dry? Give the reader a sense of what's to come. As you advance the story, establish guideposts where you can set up a theme or throughline that will allow the delivery to be meaningful and funny. It may be helpful to begin with the end, i.e. the punchline, in mind. This will help you understand how to encapsulate the entire joke in a manner that feels cohesive. By working backward, you can reverse engineer the thought process so that you start exactly where you need to be to get where you want to go without any extraneous deviations that may muddle the message.

DEVELOPING LIFE INTO A STORY

Another method for developing story ideas is to start with an element from your life and tailor it to fit the personalities of your characters. Keep in mind, comedy doesn't need to be elaborate with a lot of props, bells, and whistles. Don't be afraid to keep it simple by getting personal and sharing aspects of yourself because the relatability creates a connection with the audience. The laughter comes from the reader's recognition of themselves in you and your work.

If you're writing about yourself in the form of an essay or memoir, self-deprecation is a viable option for creating humor. Making fun of yourself or examining your personal attributes can create universal ties to the way others conduct themselves and thus ingratiate you and your work to the audience. Use your own physical, emotional, and psychological struggles as a means of exploring the humor inherent in our collective anxieties. You get more laughs when the audience recognizes themselves in your joke. Talk show host and podcaster Conan O'Brien is a master at relatability through self-deprecation.

Use the questions below to examine the meaningful moments of your life and see if you can incorporate those behaviors or events into a story. Again, this is not necessarily about recreating those scenarios verbatim but rather using them as the foundation for something new.

- Is there a situation from your life that's funny or ridiculous—perhaps in retrospect?
- What aspect of life always blows your mind? Is there

something about your daily routine you can't stand, like the lady at the deli who smells all the bagels before making her selection? Your inspiration point doesn't need to start off teeming with comedy as long as it contains a relatable element, which you can use as the foundation on which to build the laughs.
- Have I created a situation that can be interpreted more than one way? This leaves room to subvert expectations and create an unexpected punchline or conclusion.
- Is there a way to utilize dramatic irony to help create tension and suspense prior to the punchline?

Continue to expand upon these basic ideas. Ask yourself: What happens next? Why? How did we get from Point A to Point B, and how does the result of that initial journey affect the next step?

CRAFTING COMEDIC STORYLINES

Stories are all about obstacles. Therefore, your lead characters can't walk into the story fully formed as perfect human beings. They need to be messy, misguided, broken, delusional, or just plain bad. Those are the kind of people who tend to learn lessons from the dilemmas they face. Don't worry too much about the audience disliking them. They simply need to be relatable and complex enough to seem real.

The story flourishes when your characters figure out a way to grow or learn something in the face of conflict. No one wants to read a story where the protagonist is perfect in every way. We want to relate to them through their struggles. Also, think about ways to end your story with a touch of hope. People want stories with hope because hope implies a better future and that makes people happy. Hope and love are ultimately what life is about.

People read stories to see themselves reflected, so base your stories on the trials and the tribulations of the human ego, not self-righteousness or perfect morals. Every character should have gray areas, even the good guys.

In comedy, introduce each new character with a bang. Not only does this allow for a memorable personality trait that helps the audience remember the players throughout the story, it is an opportunity to provide laughs organically without the effort feeling forced. Consider this example from *Clouds Atlas* (2004) by David Mitchell:

> "Good morning," began the woman.
>
> "I beg to differ."
>
> "My name is Gwendolin Bendincks."
>
> "Don't blame me."

Even though this breaks the rule of no small talk it does serve the purpose of establishing a baseline characterization and tone for the scene. It also provides some unexpected humor.

As you become more familiar with these concepts, don't write a story with the expectation that the punchline will do the heavy lifting. A reader can always tell when they are being strung along in that regard. Just like an article feels preachy when you build it around a moral mandate or a mystery feels stilted when you build a scene around exposing a clue, humor fails to deliver when you craft the story around a laugh. The comedic elements should come from the collective forces of the characters, setting, dialogue, and theme. Pull any one of those things out and the humor should deflate.

Don't pander to the reader simply to gain quick laughs. If you're not familiar with the term, pandering is to provide what someone wants or demands even though it is not necessarily in good taste or in line with the surrounding content. When a comic goes on stage and starts their act with a quick joke about the local football team just to make the audience cheer (even though he or she has no real interest or opinion about sports), that's pandering. Granted, this is a fairly mild example, but the point is that it's disingenuous and far too easy to rely on that kind of humor. Be smarter and work to surprise the audience rather than cater to their basic instincts.

Don't force laughs, earn them.

DRAMATIC VERSUS COMEDIC DIALOGUE

The difference between dramatic and comedic characters is their mental focus. Yes, both protagonists are in pursuit of an essential desire. However, while the dramatic character learns from each challenge and recalculates his approach, the comedic character races ahead with the same self-absorbed obsession over and over, expecting different results. In essence, what makes a comedic character humorous is his inability to see beyond his initial choices. We watch him struggle, and we laugh knowing we would never be so naive. We take a lesson from his hardships and root for him to break his pattern one day. Michael Scott (Steve Carell), from the American sitcom *The Office* (2005), is an example of such a person.

But with that said, the comedic protagonist should not be mistaken for a mere cipher. His goals and motivations are couched in a fully formed characterization complete with fears, morals, values, speech patterns, and expectations. This character is an autonomous being except for that ongoing obsession. Thus, it is within that dichotomy between objective person and obsessed person that the comedy is found. The comic character is often played as an exaggeration so that we can see this distinction more clearly, and his stories are often told with a little more psychic distance than usual, allowing the reader to play the role of judge and jury when the protagonist's ludicrous behavior extends beyond society's norms.

But what does this mean in terms of creating artful dialogue? Three things: First, humor isn't just about what the character says, it's also how he says it and how he reacts in connection with it. Second, these reactions are an exaggeration of the emotions the character feels. Third, these feelings are the result of strong desires toward a goal that the character is willing to pursue unceasingly. Therefore, just as we noted at the start of this chapter, it is important that you adequately know your characters before you craft your comic dialogue.

HUMOR DEFINITIONS

Before we wrap up, let's outline the definitions for some of the basic forms of humor:

Farce is a form of slapstick comedy where everything is absurd, usually in a lewd or exaggerated manner. The storylines often appeal to the audience's baser instincts and may involve deception, miscommunication, and mistaken identity. A modern example is the American television series *Three's Company* (1977), and a classic example is Oscar Wilde's play *The Importance of Being Earnest* (1899).

Parodies imitate, comment upon, or make fun of something or someone while exaggerating the features for comic effect. This is a humorous way to point out the flaws in something or to dig into a problem in a lighthearted manner. A well-executed parody should be funny regardless of whether the audience has seen the work being imitated. You may also hear parodies referred to as **spoofs**. We see these a lot on *YouTube* and *Saturday Night Live*, but an example of a literary parody is *Pride and Prejudice and Zombies* (2009) by Seth Grahame-Smith.

Satire strives to do more than entertain. The goal is to place a spotlight on corrupt ideas or institutions through ridicule, irony, or exaggeration in order to inform the audience and make them think. A modern example is the comic strip *Calvin and Hobbs* (1985) created by Bill Watterson, and a classic example is the novella *Animal Farm* (1945) by George Orwell. Similarly, a **lampoon** is "a harsh satire usually directed against an individual," according to *Merriam Webster Online*.

HUMOR WRITING CHECKLIST

- Is the pacing tight? Is there a nice balance of dramatic and light-hearted moments? Are there places where the audience might lose interest? Figure out why and endeavor to fix them.
- Do all of the humorous bits serve the narrative by either providing characterization or moving the story forward?
- Do the humorous lines feel authentic to each character?
- Do all the jokes work as intended? Make sure the audience is laughing with the joke, not at the amateurishness of the execution.
- Did I end each scene with either a laugh, an action, a resolution to take action, or a resonating image?

Even if 90 percent of the story works that uneven 10 percent can topple the whole enterprise, so resolve to seek counsel on your work through a critique group or hired editor. Then do your best to apply the relevant feedback, especially if the same note is received from two or more different sources.

Exercise: Humor

Exercise #1: Observe the world around you. Keep a notebook handy to record anything that makes you laugh. This can be a turn of phrase you hear on the street, pet peeves, accents, or attitude shifts. As you develop your work in progress, review your notebook. Look for funny elements or idiosyncrasies that speak to the universal aspects of what it means to be human. Add them to your story in places where the humor will help develop your character or those sections where the mood needs to be lightened after a dark turn or revelation.

Exercise #2: Identify an amusing, unorthodox, embarrassing, or challenging event or behavior from your life. Then imagine a character for whom this would be the worst-case scenario. What obstacles would they face? What would this person do to cope? What aspects of this person's personality would exacerbate the situation? Design the event to deliver maximum conflict and, hence, potential for comedy. Work to create a story that is powerful and cohesive enough that it would work even if the jokes were removed. Give the work purpose and a reason to exist. Also, keep the stakes— i.e. what the protagonist stands to gain or lose—high so the audience feels for your character.

Exercise #3: List three things that make you laugh. Use the 5Ws of writing—who, what, where, when, and why—to brainstorm a scene using all three elements. Try to distill the funny aspects of that scene down to a single paragraph that contains a setup, reversal, and punchline. Keep in mind, humor lives in the space between the expected and the unexpected. This smattering of unpredictability can turn the mundane into something magical.

Exercise #4: Examine one your favorite comedic characters. What wordplay, catchphrases, or physical attributes made this person hilariously memorable? What literary devices did the writer use to create comedy? Is the humor found more in the setting and situation than the character's actual behavior? Use your observations as inspiration for infusing more humor into your work.

Exercise #5: Write a humorous short story using the techniques discussed in this chapter. Give the manuscript cohesive beginning, middle, and conclusion, but it must open and close with the same line of dialogue.

Exercise #6: Find a play that you enjoy. Select a scene from the work that isn't comic. Observe the characters' goals, motives, and physicality and see if you can turn the situation into comedic one. You may need to change or eliminate some things to make this work. For example, the conflict or closing disaster may need to be exaggerated to induce a more comical effect. Experiment with the tools you've learned so far to craft a humorous scene that keeps the original essence.

Exercise #7: We often see self-deprecating comedy in fiction because the character can use it as coping or defense mechanism. To practice this technique, create a list of personal qualities—both physical and social—that would make excellent comedic fodder. Using the list, write at least three jokes one of your characters could tell about himself.

Exercise #8: Find a work of art that touches you—it can be a painting, book, film, or podcast. Look for something about it that conjures deep emotions like, in the case of romance or tragedy, the need to weep. Pinpoint the exact moment that brings about those feelings and examine what occurred to elicit that response. Is the character immensely honest? Is the writer using strong verbs? Is the character broken and fighting against insurmountable odds? Has the author used metaphor and simile to create a hyperbole? Once you understand what you're drawn to about the work, write down your findings and attempt to incorporate those techniques into your next writing endeavor.

Pro Tip: Save your alternate jokes and ideas. Even though that material may not work in the present moment, it could be revamped and used during revision or spawn a completely separate idea that stands as its own work of art. Do this by maintaining a secondary document that will accompany the different drafts of your text. Make note which scene the material was originally meant to cover and how you came up with the idea, especially if that concept was sparked by a real-life person, place, or thing. This will give you the freedom to play around with what humorous scenarios work best as your move toward publication.

Inflammatory Language

Inflammatory language is defined as words that incite anger or disorder.

- **Profanity** – a disregard for what's sacred; e.g. "You don't know a God damn thing about me!" or "Jesus H. Christ!"
- **Cursing** – an obscenity that expresses the desired misfortune of another; e.g. "Screw you and the horse you rode in on!"
- **Swearing** – coarse or vulgar language found offensive in polite society; aka those forbidden four letter words like "You cock sucking cunt."
- **Ethnophaulisms** – derogatory, pejorative, hostile, or insulting terms used toward an ethnic group or race

At some point, you'll need to make a decision about whether you plan to incorporate one or more of these categories into your story.

To be clear, if hurtful or offensive language is appropriate to the historical time period you're using, this fact doesn't mean you should automatically use those words. Similarly, if you've created a dastardly character, this doesn't always warrant foul phrases.

When making a decision about racial epithets and swear words first consider if that language actually brings something to your text in terms of advancing the plot, complicating conflict, or developing character. If you can honestly answer in the affirmative to all three elements, ask yourself: Is this the only way to gain those results?

Some traditional publishers believe that foul language has the potential to affect sales and prefer that authors forgo using those words in hopes of capturing a larger audience. And of course, there are genres, like cozies and sweet romance, where audiences expect the text to remain clean.

If you still think it is important to incorporate those terms, tread lightly. Keep your usage to a minimum, and be strategic about your placement. When in doubt, discuss the situation with your editor or with people like your beta and sensitivity readers who may be able to articulate why such language could be offensive.

Bottomline: You don't want to put anything in your novel that might dilute the overall message. Remember all the flack Quentin Tarantino received over *Django Unchained* (2012)? If the incorporation of foul language overshadows all the other great themes and ideas you hope to convey, maybe it is better to avoid the usage.

If you choose to split the difference and use substitutes for foul language, make sure your selections support the tone and mood you desire. In other words, don't use "fiddlesticks" as a swear in a gritty cop drama because it will evoke laughs from the audience, which probably isn't your intention. Instead, craft euphemisms that properly reflect the genre and your characters. For instance, that gritty cop could start to swear but always be cut off mid-phrase by his partner who is the keeper of the precinct's swear jar. That way, the character's verbal intentions are restricted by a contextual device that feels believable while still creating what sounds like real life dialogue.

Also, keep in mind that expletives are often loud and obnoxious when spoken. They are quick bursts of energy that take the air out of the room. So maybe you'd rather replace those naughty terms with an action, which gives you the option to develop a quieter version of that inflammatory moment or have that reaction slowly crescendo to its explosion. For instance, rather than use profanity, maybe your character kicks things or punches walls. That reaction can ebb or surge if there isn't a wall in the immediate vicinity, which can be something fun to play with as you write.

Overall, there are no official rules when it comes to harsh language. Do what feels right for you and your book's genre. You can always write your rough draft with foul language then take the references out when you better understand your story's focus and your genre's ideal reader.

Historical Language

Writing historical language is like spinning plates. You must provide enough history and culture that the speech seems authentic, but you also need to be cognizant of creating language that's accessible to the modern audience while also well-paced and entertaining—all without backsliding into contemporary slang.

This requires a ton of research, patience, and meticulousness. Consider joining these organizations to help your quest:

- Historical Writers' Association - https://historicalwriters.org/
- Historical Novel Society - https://historicalnovelsociety.org/
- A Writer of History (author M.K. Tod's site focusing on writing and researching historical fiction) - https://awriterofhistory.com/

Luckily, our digital world makes it easy to search online or Skype with a historian about the speech patterns, mindset, dress, and economic status of the various social classes during the Elizabethan Era. But if it is a recent period like the 1950s or 1970s, you may also want to go to your local library to see if you can retrieve some periodicals or literature to get a better sense of the language. Plays, advertisements, society notices, and catalogs are also an option. And even though television is a different medium, it may help to watch shows, films, and documentaries from the period to experience the cadence of speech from speakers of that time. For older settings like Middle Ages, your research may become more academically inclined, so university libraries may prove more helpful in that regard.

FIVE STEPS TO CREATING HISTORICAL DIALOGUE

- Curate a list of the historical words—idioms, objects, greetings, slang, et cetera—needed to enrich the setting of your story.
- Determine areas of the text where such language can be utilized. Limit yourself to three to four phrases per scene. The idea is that you introduce the new terms gradually and in small doses to avoid overwhelming the reader.
- Ensure the setting and context are clear so that you can provide the meaning for your new words through the character's behavior and the scene's action. You want to avoid having to stop to explain terms since that may turn into info dumping. Incorporate words using gentle repetition, and try to pair them with recognizable terms or concepts to enhance meaning.
- Check for anachronisms or elements that may be chronologically unfit for the time period. Readers are willing to suspend disbelief in terms of the plot, but you want to avoid obvious mistakes in language, especially if the period is recent enough to easily research such as 1950s slang versus today.

Your dialogue should reflect the period you're emulating without being stilted. That is to say, don't let your quest for authenticity result in scenes that are cumbersome, dull, and poorly paced. Gradually add historical words or phrases so that the effect is unobtrusive but powerful. Remember, your goal isn't to develop a historical facsimile, it's to create relatable characters who are believable. Your historical language should feel credible while still appealing to the sensibilities of a modern audience.

Accents, Dialects, & Foreign Languages

Dialogue is your opportunity to play with language and have fun. You don't need to use perfect grammar all the time. In fact, if you're getting the note that your work sounds stuffy, stiff, or stilted, it's possible that your writing doesn't reflect how people talk.

Even though you may feel obligated to maintain some level of formality for the narrative descriptions, you're ultimately free to have your characters' dialogue utilize contractions, split infinitives, double negatives, run-on sentences, or whatever grammar rules you see fit to break.

In real life, people speak in fragments, change topics suddenly, drop words, and shorten phrases, and you have the option to do the same as long as the choices continue to add to the characterization and propel plot. You can also add another layer to your dialogue by incorporating accents, dialects, slang, jargon, and other languages. This chapter will show you how.

Accents

The word *accent* refers to how words are pronounced or how they sound. But in literary terms, think of an accent as someone's distinctive inflection, rhythm, and tone.

Accents in English can be denoted with an occasional phonetic spelling, but be careful of this. You don't want the usage to become so cartoonish that it borders on offensive. You also don't want the oddity of the language to distract the reader from the meaning.

> "Hey deh, Suga. Yousa prehtay yung thang 'rite deh now, eh?"

It's often more effective to play the line straight and simply add a colloquialism that helps the reader hear the inflections.

"Hey there, Suga. You a pretty young thing now, eh?"

As an alternative to trying to write the sounds and inflections of an accent, use atypical word order or incorporate the grammar constructions that are often associated with non-native English speakers. For example, Russian doesn't use verbs in the same manner as English. Linking verbs like *to be* aren't actively incorporated because they are implied. Therefore, a sentence like *Here is your money* may translate in its accented form as *Here your money*. Similarly, some of the other Slavic languages rarely use articles like *a, an,* and *the*, so *Look at the issue* can become *Look at issue*.

"There is much things wrong with what you say."

"You want me to give you the trouble?"

"What is the time?"

With a technique like this, you get the feel of accented speech without concocting strange words and spellings that may alienate your audience and make the text difficult to read.

Also, sometimes something as simple as eliminating contractions can give the effect of an accent since most native English speakers rely on short word forms while many ESL speakers shy away from them. For example:

"I am so happy we are having you in our home."

Again, just make sure that your attempts to describe the accent or speech of a character whose native tongue differs from yours doesn't come off as patronizing or mocking. The goal is to create dialogue that's believable and recognizable and complimentary to the characterization.

If you don't feel comfortable with these approaches, then keep it simple. Ask for help from a language expert or someone who utilizes the accent you want to emulate. Or if push comes to shove, just tell the audience and let them use their imagination.

> Astrid shouted in a thick Swedish accent. "Keep away from the windows."

Lastly, sometimes a character's accented speech is revealed through their efforts to assimilate into a new group. You can have them misunderstanding or misusing common idioms and colloquialisms as a way to show their accent. Or their incorrect word choices and pronunciation could be noticed by others as off-kilter and become the element that exposes that character as an outsider. For example, consider these lines from *Coming to America* (1988). This is an excerpt of the scene where Akeem (Eddie Murphy) attempts to impress his boss (John Amos), who happens to also be the father of a woman he wishes to date.

AKEEM

Sir, I was wondering, did you happen to catch the professional football contest on television last night?

MR. MCDOWELL

No, I didn't.

AKEEM

Oh, it was most exhilarating. The Giants of New York took on the Packers of Green Bay, and in the end the Giants triumphed by kicking an oblong ball made of pigskin through a big 'H.' It was a most ripping victory.

MR. MCDOWELL

Son, I'm just gonna tell you this one time.

AKEEM

Yes, sir?

Mr. MCDOWELL

You want to keep working here, stay off the drugs.

This exchange is obviously written for the screen and played for comic effect since Zamunda isn't a real African country, but it is a decent example of how to reveal an accent without contorting the words you choose to place on the page.

Dialects

According to *Merriam-Webster Dictionary Online*, dialect is "a regional variety of language distinguished by features of vocabulary, grammar, and pronunciation." The telltale word here is *regional* because dialects are often thought of as the various forms of language used by members of a specific region, social group, or class. If you're confused about how dialects differ from accents, just keep in mind that the accent is mainly about the pronunciation while dialect encompasses not only the sound but also the diction, grammar, usage, and syntax.

Every country and language has various dialects. For instance, in the United States, dialects deal with regions like The Deep South or Long Island, New York. It is also worth noting that social class and status sometimes determines dialect. Consider the posh idioms and lockjaw accent used by billionaire Thurston Howell III (Jim Backus) on Gilligan's Island (1964) to highlight his position as an elitist Newport, Rhode Island resident and card-carrying Republican.

No matter which locale your dialect represents, start by making a list of colloquialisms, slang, or regionalisms to help with the depiction. Try to go beyond examples found in your favorite film or what you think you know about a place. Visit when you can or find people from the area to interview. Look for news broadcasts or local special interest shows that may provide insight into what that dialect sounds like under everyday circumstances.

Again, be cautious when writing dialect or representing an accent. Although you may be composing things phonetically to suit the ear, this doesn't always translate to something that's pleasing to the mind's eye. Remember, readers pay more attention to the dialogue than the narrative, so any annoying elements of dialect are magnified. Taking dialect too far may wear out your reader. The key is to suggest dialect, not duplicate it.

The Known World (2003) by Edward P. Jones is a prime example of dialect done well. The novel is set in Virginia during the antebellum era and examines the moral implications of slavery.

> "Don't know bout no buryin, Marse," Stennis said of the child Abundance, "gettin them chains off and on. Watchin em so they don't run away. Lotta trouble for somethin that won't cause no more trouble in this world."

Notice how Jones practices restraint in demonstrating dialect by simply dropping one or two letters from a few words. Nothing is so egregiously misspelled or made up that it pulls us out of the text. Every spelling change is common enough that the dialect is perfectly rendered without sacrificing readability or morphing into an offensive stereotype.

The words chosen as well as their order help us understand with what cadence the language should be spoken and the speaker's social status.

If you'd like to read the work of other writers who craft excellent dialect, consider Andrea Levy, Gloria Naylor, Zora Neale Hurston, Hilary Mantel, Junot Diaz, Alice Walker, Sherman Alexie, Alice Walker, Sapphire, Toni Morrison, Amy Tan, Gus Lee, Earl Lovelace, and Sara Waters.

In addition, be mindful that when we add dialect to dialogue, there is a slight reduction of pace. The reader slows to pay a little more attention to what the character means by their words and phrases, so be mindful that when you use this technique, you're essentially putting a spotlight on your character. Thus, you may want to avoid heavy dialect or accents for people you want to go unnoticed like the killer in a mystery.

At the end of the day, what's most important about dialects and accents is that a) you're employing them respectfully and b) you have a specific reason for the usage. To guarantee that you've covered both bases, ask yourself the following questions:

- Does my use of accents or dialects serve a vital story purpose?
- Have I kept my usage of accents or dialects to a minimum?
- Has the use of accents or dialects included any offensive words, expressions, or phrases that I should tone down, further contextualize, or remove?
- Have I used my accents or dialects to aid in characterization?

In short, every dialect and accent is based on a logic that must be consistently respected in order to work, and this chapter gives you a number of frameworks to follow. However, don't feel obligated to create dialects or accents for the sake of authenticity. Audiences are more than willing to suspend disbelief and imagine those elements if you simply tell them a character has one.

Foreign Languages

If you want to include passages of a foreign language in your text, one option is to convey the character's dialogue in English, but make it clear that they are speaking another language based on the narrative or the reactions of the people around them. You can also have the text's descriptive elements comment on the sound of the language. For example:

> He rolled his "R" with a snarky flourish.
>
> She snarled at us in a fierce hiss of German. "Get off my lawn."

If you'd like to see an example of this in action, David Sedaris does an excellent job of this in his humorous essay "Jesus Shaves" from the collection *Me Talk Pretty One Day* (2000) where he chronicles learning French and his experience of living in France without knowing the language.

But how do we represent the voice of a character who doesn't speak English at all or who occasionally needs to speak a foreign language?

One option is to write the character's lines in the desired language then repeat the translation in English or vice versa. We see this technique used all the time in music.

> "Qué será, será. Whatever will be, will be."

This method works best when the passages are short. Also, don't overdo it. You don't want to get in the habit of writing everything twice. Therefore, another approach to consider is to simply add a foreign phrase to each response to give the essence of another language being spoken.

"Me llamo Renaldo Sanchez. Bienvenida a mi casa. Make yourself comfortable."

If you need additional ideas, *Bel Canto* (2001) by Ann Patchett is a great example of a fiction work where references to Japanese, French, Spanish, and Russian are handled adeptly via the dialogue without confusing the reader or diminishing the power of any language. The story is told in English and chronicles the poignant relationships built among a group of international investors taken hostage by terrorists during a birthday celebration where a famous American opera singer was set to perform. As suggested by the title, this plot skews more romantic than its thrilling premise would suggest. Also, I should note the book's events are loosely based on the 1996 embassy hostage crisis in Lima, Peru.

Resources: Accents. Dialects, & Foreign Languages

All things considered, it is best to work with a native speaker—or better yet, a group of people—who know the accent, dialect, language, or jargon you want to incorporate in your dialogue. Try to meet with them personally or online, rather than over the phone, so that you can also keep track of the gestures and body language they use accompany their words. This will help bring the essence of realism to your work.

If you have trouble connecting with someone, try the Center for Applied Linguistics Collection found on the Library of Congress website:

http://memory.loc.gov/ammem/collections/linguistics

The collection consists of 118 audio hours of North American dialects via speech samples, interviews, and oral histories.

In addition, there are a number of desk references that you can utilize like travel guides and the various foreign language dictionaries. Random House, Penguin, and Macmillan all have dictionaries on historical slang if you're willing to search the web for used copies (none of them are currently in print). With that said, here are a few other resources to help inspire your research:

- *A New Look at Old Words: Street Slang from the 1600s – 1800s: A Writer's Categorized Guide* by Catherine Thrush
- *The Great Book of American Idioms: A Dictionary of American Idioms, Sayings, Expressions, & Phrases* by Lingo Mastery
- *British English from A to Zed: A Definitive Guide to the Queen's English* by Norman W. Schur
- *A History of the English Language* by Albert C. Baugh and Thomas Cable
- *The Oxford English Dictionary of Etymology* edited by C.T. Onions, G.W.S. Friedrichsen, & R.W. Burchfield
- *Urban Dictionary* - https://www.urbandictionary.com/

Exercise: Accents, Dialects, & Foreign Languages

Exercise: Select a scene you've already written and reimagine it using a dialect you've researched. To find the right balance, you will rewrite the scene three times. When you write the scene the first time, exaggerate your spellings and phrasing to mimic the dialect's sound. This may involve phonetic spellings or elisions. When you write the scene the second time, maintain normal spellings and phrasing. Instead, let your word choice and the overall sentence structure to hint at the dialect. Once you've finished, review both versions, and take the best elements from each to create the third version of your scene. Where does the language best mimic the dialect's rhythm? Are there idioms, words, or sayings particular to the culture that you can lightly add to help the reader better hear what's being spoken?

Slang

Slang is informal diction that's often dictated by popular culture. Some examples that have stood the test of time include: cool, awesome, dude, sweet, dope, wicked, and bad (meaning good).

If you're writing a contemporary book, avoid overdosing on slang. Most of it doesn't age well, and its use will date your material. The meaning of words in general, but slang in particular, tends to morph over time or fall out of fashion (RIP *on fleek*), so choose wisely.

If you don't believe me, consider how *troll* and *catfish*, once proud nouns, have transitioned into verbs over the last ten years. Or better yet, imagine how weird a fad-based nonsense word like *yeet* may feel by the time your work reaches the bestseller list. Remember, traditionally published books often take a year to go to press. Therefore, what starts as a hip reference, may seem awkward by the time the book hits print.

Indie authors should also beware—yes, self-published books come to market much faster, but they also stay on the shelf longer, leaving room for slang to fall out of fashion. Since we don't know what will resonate as the years progress, it's best to avoid anything too trendy.

Instead, strive instead for innovation. Look for evergreen ways to keep your dialogue trending or devise a way of speaking that's congruent with the new world you've built for the characters in your book. This will not only make your work unique but also open the door for dialogue that's catchy, quotable, and memorable enough to enter the zeitgeist in its own right. J.K. Rowling was a wizard at this (play on words intended!), devising terms like *muggle*, *splinching* (split + pinching), and *patronus* (this last one is a very clever appropriation of the ancient Roman concept of a physical protector).

In order to create new words that convey their own meaning, a practice known as neologism, you'll need to have a clear understanding of the culture you've created and your characters' behavior within it. You don't want your futuristic space society sounding like the teenagers of today, and you don't want all the races on your new planet to sound exactly the same.

As you're formulating dialogue, don't weigh down each speech with words and phrases your readers won't comprehend. Slowly introduce new concepts and repeat them so that their meaning and importance to the culture become an intuitive part of the reader's consciousness. It also helps if the terms you create are slight variations of words the audience may already know. One way is to use foreign language dictionaries, dead language spellings (e.g. Old Norse), or the early-English version of words. You can even modify common terms by creating an alternative spelling or adding punctuation to invent your own version of a language that still has a readable and relatable feel.

To stay organized, you may want to keep a list of vocabulary words, similar to a style sheet, to remind yourself of how certain characters speak and what expressions they typically use. This will help maintain consistency throughout the book. A style sheet is simply a document that lists the grammar and usage choices you made during your writing journey.

If you story isn't fantasy or science fiction, you can still use the aforementioned approach. Consider films like *Wayne's World* (1992), *Clueless* (1995), and *Mean Girls* (2004) or novels like *A Clockwork Orange* (1962) by Anthony Burgess—they all contain their own slang and the language works within the reality-based world the authors created.

Still not convinced? Let's discuss Oscar-nominated screenwriter and novelist Richard Price, who invented some of the slang for his fifth novel, *Clockers* (1992). According to a 1992 review in *The New York Times*,

Price devised the term after several ride-alongs with narcotics officers. He wanted a word that evoked the imagery of drug dealers being on the street around the clock without "... trying to be au courant by picking up the rapology of the moment, because by the time it's in print it's lost its resonance." He also noted that "knockos," a slang term for cops in the novel, came from his initial misinterpretation of drug dealers calling their nemeses "narcos."

The point here is to think outside the box. Rather than relying on trends, dig into the language and make it your own. But with that said, if you are writing a historical, by all means use the slang of the era because it will help lend believability and naturalism to the dialogue as well as provide a brief history lesson for the audience.

On a different but similar note, make sure to use catchphrases and idiolects in moderation. This includes slang, idioms, and affectations like *darling* or *ya'll*. As we've been noting throughout, overuse detracts from the reader's understanding of the text and muddles the pacing of the narrative. So use them sparingly or only apply such elements to one or two of the main characters in a manner that helps us to better understand their backstory and who they are as people.

Lastly, ensure each use of slang is distinct to the individual. You don't want characters swapping personal sayings or mannerism—unless it is the single-use payoff to a joke that has been built up over an extended portion of the story. Think *Back to the Future III* (1990) when Marty McFly and Doc Brown switch their famous catchphrases: "This is heavy," and "Great Scott!"

Phone Conversations

Phone conversations can be complicated to navigate succinctly because they lend themselves to the inclusion of extraneous information like greetings, valedictions, small talk, et cetera. To avoid this, structure the scene so that your characters focus on the primary purpose for the exchange. Save any important internal dialogue for the moments after the conclusion of the call. This will ensure the scene maintains a steady pace. Basically, we don't want to linger too long on a phone call because it limits the opportunity for action.

In fact, if it is possible to forgo the telephone altogether by summarizing all or part of the conversation via indirect dialogue, then that's the tactic you should take. This will allow you to underscore the portion of the conversation that's most relevant to the reader. Consider the examples below:

Sample phone conversation – Full Indirect Dialogue

> I put my cellphone on speaker while Daphne confessed she'd cheated on Mike . . . again. She also admitted she had no plans to break up with him because they had a trip to Hawaii planned for their anniversary. My response was brutal.

Sample phone conversation – Partial Indirect Dialogue + Direct Dialogue

> After spending twenty minutes listening to Tess gossip about her latest affair in the same breath as her tenth anniversary trip, I couldn't take it anymore. "How can you be so fucking cavalier about someone's feelings? Shit or get off the pot."

Regardless of your approach, remember to keep the conversation moving. Don't waste moments of the telephone exchange explaining why the characters are calling. Those explanations should have been provided in the scenes prior to the call or from the context of the call itself. If the content of your pleasantries and idle chit-chat does not add anything major to the characterizations or conflict, cut them and transition directly into the main dialogue. Begin in a place where the conversation has already gained its momentum. It also helps to keep the characters active throughout the conversation by using vocal descriptions, pauses, or action beats. Here is an example from *Poetic Justice*, my cozy courthouse mystery series:

> I dialed Grace's number and crossed my fingers she'd answer at such a late hour. Four rings later, I had a cranky, husky-voiced Grace on the line.
>
> I plunged into my request without preamble. "Do you think you could get me a copy of the surveillance footage you gave Detective Daniels?"
>
> "Well, good evening to you too." She yawned. "Thanks for waking me to make sure my phone works. I'm going to hang up now."
>
> "Grace, I'm serious. If I can just get a look at that footage, I might be able to wrap my head around Ms. Freddie's death."
>
> "Fine." She huffed. "For Freddie. Friday. After work. My office. Tell no one. Me sleep now."
>
> Friday? That was two whole days away. Much later than I'd hoped...

The call has ended. No hangups. No goodbyes. The scene continues with the viewpoint character pondering the consequences of having to wait for the urgent information she needs. Notice how those thoughts were saved until after the phone call? Moreover, consider how the setup and the dialogue manages to forgo the normal opening filler by giving the characters a scene-based motive for wanting to complete the call as quickly as possible. There is also a bit of sarcastic tension between the women even though they are allies. All of these tactics are wonderful ways for creating calls that are clever and concise.

Also, don't forget that when the viewpoint character is the person engaging in the phone call, we're in their head, so you can show both sides of the conversation regardless of what POV is being used. It's only when the viewpoint character is listening to someone else talk on the phone that the overheard conversation would need to be one-sided.

But overall, it probably best to limit the number of phone calls in your novel because you don't want numerous scenes where the actors aren't able to interact face to face, which minimizes your ability to have actions and gestures that feed the conflict.

Jargon

Stories involving science or advance technology may require the use of jargon in the dialogue. Jargon is specialized terminology used by people in a particular profession—e.g. medicine, aviation, computer science, military, law, et cetera. Jargon is an excellent opportunity to introduce your readers to a new vocabulary, profession, culture, and a pattern of banter they might not otherwise experience.

Even though you may not share your character's training, it is important to faithfully recreate how the language is employed within the discipline. But be mindful, sometimes the jargon's daily reality is different from the version found in your research. For example, a busy emergency room doctor talking to her colleagues probably wouldn't say *atrial fibrillation* even though that's the correct jargon for her field. She'd more likely say AFib since most medical professionals shorten common phrases in the essence of time. In other words, it is not enough simply to know the jargon, you must also understand how it's used in the community.

Fortunately, the difficult part of incorporating jargon into your writing isn't usage. That's something you can easily learn by immersing yourself in the profession and finding the proper experts to assist you. The big problem is that once you use jargon, how do you clarify meaning without stalling your story's pace with a huge information dump? In other words, how do you explain it, without explaining it?

I would argue that if you're writing with a clear purpose, your scene's setting, conflict, and stakes should provide enough context for the reader's understanding. Let the dialogue and action flow. Trust that your audience will be able to figure things out through the full sequence of events. *Reversible Errors* (2002) by Scott Turow is a great example of how to use police jargon without bogging down the exchange with definitions that would slow the pace. In this excerpt, a cop and a security guard discuss an arrest:

> "He's over in County."
>
> "The jail or the hospital?"
>
> "Crossbars Motel."
>
> "For?"
>
> "Buy-bust."
>
> "How much?"
>
> "Six zones as they say." Six ounces. "Class X."
>
> "That's tough."
>
> "Terrible tough. This'll make him Triple X." Triple X, three felony convictions for narcotics, would mean life in prison unless he could offer something to prosecutors.

"He'll have to find his tongue."

Notice that the text is very lean, and the author dispenses with dialogue tags because the question-and-answer rhythm helps the reader easily identify each speaker. In addition, Turow uses the narrative to explain anything the reader is unable to pick up through context, but he keeps it brief to maintain the pace.

If the jargon is extremely complex, you may want to have an expert explain the information to a novice character who will ask questions and force the speaker to slow down. Another method is to have a highly knowledgeable layman (e.g. ex-scientist, ex-cop) introduce the information in simple terms. The idea is that this person is highly familiar with the technical talk but doesn't feel obligated to use it—or may even be resentful or tired of it—so they make a point of dumbing down their explanation.

Ghostbusters (1984) is one of my favorite movies and, even though it's a comedy that hinges on fake science, the scenes where Dr. Egon Spengler explains things to new hire Winston Zeddemore are basic examples of this technique.

A third alternative would involve the narrator or viewpoint character summarizing the concept or idea, noting that the explanation may have taken them some time to grasp or may have been boring but here is what they've come to understand about the situation and here is what they need to do next for the story to move forward.

The point is that if and when you choose to explain jargon, it shouldn't feel technical. If it helps, put the focus on the consequences of the procedure, product, or event so that emotion is pulled to the forefront of the situation. The definition becomes *less* about the inner workings of the device and the jargon that goes along with it and *more* about how that object or idea plays into the larger story question.

Jargon can be tricky, but it has the potential to increase the story's realism and add an air of authenticity to your characters.

Point of View

Whose story is this? What point of view am I telling it from?

The decision between first and third person is about how you'd like the reader to view your protagonist. Do you want the reader to see the main character objectively from a slightly outside perspective with the inner world being slowly introduced through the occasional narration that clarifies the observations made? If so, select third-person limited. Do you want to tell a sweeping epic about a large family, an apocalyptic community, a new world, or a global catastrophe? If so, select third-person omniscient. Or would you like the audience to view the main character from the inside where their subjective opinion of themselves may not match how others in the world see them? If so, select first person.

Another element to consider when selecting a viewpoint for your story is psychic distance. In *The Art of Fiction: Notes on Craft for Young Writers* (1983) by John Gardner, this term is described as the distance "...the reader feels between himself and the events of the story" (111). Understanding the audience's proximity to the viewpoint character is the key to appreciating why some books feel more immersive and why others feel more distant or why the protagonist seems more or less relatable.

- High psychic distance = the reader is detached from the story
- Low or eliminated psychic distance = the reader bonds with the story

Distant viewpoints may make it difficult to connect with the protagonist. Close viewpoints may make it difficult for the reader to gain accurate information due to personal bias. Most stories fall somewhere in the middle.

So when it comes to selecting a viewpoint character, we should pick the person most invested in the story being told. The events of the plot need to matter to them. And if your book uses several viewpoints, there should be a specific purpose for this choice—e.g. shifting time periods, star-crossed lovers, debunking an unreliable narrator, et cetera.

Here are some questions to consider when selecting a viewpoint character, whether it's for a scene or an entire novel:

- Who has the most to lose?
- Who can be present during the (scene or story) climax?
- Who gets the most out the scene?
- Who is involved in making the emotional decisions?
- Who will provide an interesting outlook or thematic spin on the story?
- Whose head are you most interested in inhabiting during the story?

Don't limit yourself to considering the most obvious characters. If you're telling a story about a widow, she doesn't necessarily need to be the only one to tell the story. The story could be told by the ghost of her husband or her children or a neighbor. What's important is finding the character who is going to illustrate the story's major points of conflict and tension.

And of course, whether you have one viewpoint character or 15 points of view like *As I Lay Dying* (1930) by William Faulkner, you should stick to one viewpoint character per scene. For example, you want to show the perspective of Adam while he's walking down the street with his date, Xavier. During their conversation, it begins to rain, so the two men take a cab. Now, since the story has changed locations, you have technically started a new scene. If you'd like to show how the date is going from Xavier's perspective, you can use this scenic shift to break into that new viewpoint. This gives you latitude to expand the audience's understanding of the date by allowing them access to the thoughts of two people without head hopping. In other words, we don't want to change viewpoints in the middle of a conversation. There should be some cue or transition that helps the audience understand that you're making a shift.

In closing, consider how different a story can be when you change viewpoints. When I discuss this topic, I always think of Rick versus Negan on *The Walking Dead* (or Thor versus Loki if you're a Millennial). Each man is the hero of his own story. They clash because they both believe they are doing the right thing. If the show (or comic) were focused on Negan rather than Rick, would our cheers go in the other direction? Food for thought.

My point is that even though this section may not directly deal with dialogue, the selection of a narrator is vital. It will affect many of your choices about the plot as well as how the reader perceives your work. Don't take it lightly.

Exercise: Point of View

Exercise: Take a scene from your work in progress and rewrite it three ways using first person, second person, and third person viewpoint. How does this change the tone of the scene? How is the voice of your main character altered? Which version has more emotion or tension? Which point of view benefited the scene the most?

Emotion in Dialogue

Every line of your story must contain emotion, but the variety and volume depend on the type of story you plan to tell and the challenges faced by your characters in the scene. Luckily, emotion unfolds in a myriad of ways. For example, anger isn't always an argument or loud voices. It is the clenched jaw, a hard stare, or a terse comment. Think of the various ways to express your characters' emotions. Use both the physical and internal. Also, remember that a person is capable of holding two contradictory emotions at once. A person can be scared and in love, angry and calm, or excited and speechless. Play around.

Weak:

"I can't believe it," grinned Tamara. "I can't believe the divorce is final."

Victor smiled. "Me either. Now we can finally be together."

This example is weak for several reasons. First, Tamara's dialogue tag is wacky. Second, the characters are discussing something they both already know simply to inform the reader. Third, the characters are telling us how they feel rather than showing us.

Strong:

"It's over." Tamara burst into a cascade of giggles. "He's really gone."

Victor slowly wrapped his arms around her waist and pulled her close. "Now I never have to let you go."

Remember, your characters' emotions not only influence what they say and how they say it, but they also affect the readers' emotions and their enjoyment of the story. In essence, emotions allow the audience to connect with your characters, so do your best to create emotive dialogue that acts as a powerful mainline for that connection.

For techniques on how to infuse emotion into your characters dialogue and behavior, invest in the Writers Helping Writers Series created by Becca Puglisi and Angela Ackerman, a couple of brilliant writing coaches known for their award-winning blog[1] of the same name. This set of books covers the various traits, moods, and tones authors use to produce memorable fiction. As of this printing, there are nine titles in the series covering everything from emotions to settings to occupations.

- *The Emotion Thesaurus*
- *The Negative Trait Thesaurus*
- *The Positive Trait Thesaurus*
- *The Rural Setting Thesaurus*
- *The Urban Setting Thesaurus*
- *The Emotional Wound Thesaurus*
- *The Occupation Thesaurus*
- *The Conflict Thesaurus* (Volume 1)
- *The Conflict Thesaurus* (Volume 2)

Mood

Mood refers to the emotions provoked in the reader from the feeling or atmosphere of a piece of literature. Establishing a mood and conveying a character's emotions through dialogue is one of the most effective ways to bring your story to life. Throughout this book, we stress and restress the importance of conflict and tension in dialogue, but we also need emotion—the character's fear, joy, doubt, et cetera—if we want to make a connection with the audience. This is the quality that makes

---

1. https://writershelpingwriters.net/blog/

the story relatable and so encourages the reader to return to your work again and again.

Figurative Language and Symbolism

Figurative language is a literary device that adds color and movement to the written word. Think of figurative language as the means to express your ideas artistically. Here are some common figurative language definitions for your reference:

- **Simile**: a comparison using "like" or "as"
- **Metaphor**: a direct comparison
- **Personification**: attributing human characteristics to something nonhuman
- **Onomatopoeia**: a word that resembles its sound (e.g. buzz, hiss, boom, pop)
- **Oxymoron**: a combination of incongruous words (e.g. small crowd, living dead, bittersweet)
- **Hyperbole**: exaggeration
- **Allusion**: a word or phrase designed to reference an outside element without explicitly mentioning it
- **Idiom**: an expression whose figurative meaning does not match its actual meaning (e.g. "I'm feeling under the weather," or "I need more cake like a whole in the head.")

Another literary device that may prove helpful to your manuscript is **symbolism**, which is when one thing represents something else. More often than not, symbols are about evoking imagery in a succinct, often subconscious manner. However, symbols can also act as stand-ins for the different facets of a character. They are also a powerful way to convey your story's theme and elicit emotion from the audience. Some common symbols in literature include the raven as a bad omen, the dove as a sign of peace, and the caged bird as a representation of innocence or isolation.

Exercise: Figurative Language and Symbolism

Exercise: Explain a complex idea like war, death, or suicide using at least one symbol and four types of figurative language. Include a viewpoint character whose dialogue will convey your ideas.

Theme

A theme is a moral or lesson that acts as the backbone for your story. By definition, themes have universal appeal—*love conquers all, what goes around comes around, there's no place like home*—so that they can easily be weaved into any tale. Most novels have at least one theme or prevailing idea whether the author is aware of it or not, but it helps to consciously select your theme in order to clarify to the audience what your story is about. A strong theme speaks to an emotional core and enhances a book's relatability. And of course, if you can plant elements of theme into your dialogue, the result will be all the more impactful for the reader.

The theme is your opportunity to make a statement about our world. What do you want to say? Keep in mind, the theme should evolve from the story you've developed. Don't shoehorn things into your work that don't fit.

However, we don't want our dialogue to reveal the theme, or central idea, in an "on the nose" manner where characters are preaching to the audience. Instead, work to convey the characters' morals and beliefs through subtext, action, and reaction. A great way to tie the theme together is to create an arc. This is something you should do at the end of your writing process once you've clearly established what your character wants and how they will evolve. But it basically involves going back to the novel's opener and crafting a scene where the character argues against the story's implied moral or lesson. That way, over the course of the book, we can better understand how they've grown. *The Wizard of Oz* (1939) is an excellent example of this.

Exercise: Theme

Exercise: Select a topic that's dear to your heart—something that would convey a message to the people around you. Summarize the idea into a single sentence—e.g. societal inequality leads to class warfare. Think about the issues that arise when people are faced with this concept, then outline what you believe is the solution, assuming one is possible. Once you've finished brainstorming, draft a scene with two characters who are on opposing sides of the issue. Over the course of the conflict, have them both learn something about the topic and themselves. This can be the resolution you devised during the brainstorm or simply a better understanding of the person on the other side of the argument. Keep in mind, your characters never need to outright state the summary sentence from earlier, but the implication should be clear from their positions. Use setting, thought, action, and symbolism to enhance meaning.

Using Dialogue to Propel the Plot

In creative writing, the plot is the set narrative events that unfold as a protagonist overcomes obstacles to achieve their goal. Or to put it another way, plot is how a story develops through conflict and characterization. A good plot is well paced and contains some level of suspense that rises to a climax over time and culminates in a resolution that rewards the reader with an emotional release. The plot also speaks to a theme that acts as the story's implied moral or lesson.

Dialogue assists the plot by providing the cast with the information they need to function within the story. Dialogue also works with the plot to identify the goals and motivations for each person while informing the reader about what's happening and what will happen next. In a nutshell, dialogue helps advance the plot—every scene works to change the current conditions for the characters so they grow closer, or further away, from their desires.

Thus, in order to write good dialogue, you must embrace the idea that every word is in service of the plot.

This does not mean that every exchange should consist solely of raw facts and data dumps designed to drive the story. How boring! Conversely, we shouldn't create characters who ramble incoherently about their lives with no aim. The key is to find the right balance. It is best to have your dialogue focus on the characters' reactions to the world as they pursue their goals. Sometimes they will be thwarted, sometimes they will be rewarded, but each outcome will teach them something new about the story problem.

Dialogue will also need to be balanced with the other elements of the plot such as setting, pacing, characterization, action, et cetera. Your job is to combine things in such a way that the plot is seamlessly integrated with the narrative elements and reminds the reader of a slice of life. Take, for example, the famous "Royale With Cheese" scene between Vincent Vega (John Travolta) and Jules Winnfield (Samuel L. Jackson) in Quentin Tarantino's *Pulp Fiction* (1994).

On the surface, it appears they are simply wasting time with a senseless debate about drugs, fast food, and foot massages. But we learn several things in that conversation that become important later in the film: 1) Vincent is an avid drug user 2) Vincent has been out of the country for several months and isn't very adventurous (or splurgy) when it comes to food 3) Both men work as muscle for a high-powered gangster named Marsellus Wallace 4) Their boss is incredibly cruel, and 5) Vincent is set to take their boss's wife out to dinner while her husband is out of town.

Plus, the interaction between the two thugs shows they're close friends and respect each other despite their obvious differences. This scene is the perfect reminder that a little bit of dialogue can go a long way in terms of informing the audience and advancing the plot.

To determine if a section of dialogue is successfully progressing your story, consider the following:

- Does the dialogue contain any elements of the theme or provide lessons that propel the characters toward the theme?
- Does this dialogue foreshadow future events, raise the stakes, increase tension, or provide suspense for the story to come?
- Does this dialogue make it clear what the character is fighting for and why it is important to them?
- Does this dialogue present a dilemma or conflict that somehow ties back to the larger story question?
- Does this dialogue challenge or change the characters in some mental, physical, or spiritual manner?
- Are there other story elements that serve the same purpose as

this section of dialogue?
- If I removed this section of dialogue, would the story remain cohesive and coherent?

Lastly, avoid isolating your characters because that lack of interaction leaves little room for growth. Naturally, there will be moments when your characters will want to do some reflection as this is often how people make decisions and create action plans for their goals. However, if a character remains in isolation, the story has nowhere to go. So when plotting your novel, be conscious about finding character interactions that are going to enhance *and progress* the story you'd like to tell.

Setting

Setting is the time and place where each scene occurs, but it also acts as the unifying element of story by tying location, time period, and culture into one milieu. Setting can convey a mood, mirror a theme, or provide an obstacle for a character's behavior. When characters use their dialogue to react to their surroundings, they are bringing setting to the forefront of the scene.

Study this excerpt from *Harry Potter and the Sorcerer's Stone* (1998) by J.K. Rowling. Can you see how setting is exposed through the dialogue? What do we learn about the space? What role does setting play in the current conflict? What hints does this setting give about conflicts to come?

> "Yes," said Professor McGonagall. "And I don't suppose you're going to tell me *why* you're here, of all places?"
>
> "I've come to bring Harry to his aunt and uncle. They're the only family he has left now."

"You don't mean—you *can't* mean the people who live *here*!" cried Professor McGonagall, jumping to her feet and pointing at number four. "Dumbledore—you can't. I've been watching them all day. You couldn't find two people who are less like us. And they've got this son—I saw him kicking his mother all the way up the street, screaming for sweets. Harry Potter come and live here!"

"It's the best place for him," said Dumbledore firmly. "His aunt and uncle will be able to explain everything to him when he's older. I've written them a letter."

"A letter?" repeated Professor McGonagall faintly, sitting back down on the wall. "Really, Dumbledore, you think you can explain all this in a letter? These people will never understand him! He'll be famous—a legend—I wouldn't be surprised if today was known as Harry Potter day in the future—there will be books written about Harry—every child in our world will know his name!"

"Exactly," said Dumbledore, looking very seriously over the top of his half-moon glasses. "It would be enough to turn any boy's head."

Even if you are too young to have familiarity with this book, it is clear from the last two lines that McGonagall and Dumbledore are from a much more civilized *world* (notice that's the word used) than the one they are currently occupying. This passage speaks volumes about setting—right down to the house number where they are standing—without resorting to things like the color of the sky or the sound of passing cars. This doesn't mean those things are unhelpful. I just want you to realize that setting can play several roles in your dialogue, including building conflict and tension. Setting is also more than just *place*; it encompass values, beliefs, professions, and cultures—even magical ones.

Bottomline: When writers fail to incorporate the environment into their dialogue, the scene feels stale. Review the techniques in this chapter to work on your approach to setting.

Start by selecting settings that aggravate the conflict already brewing in the scene so the characters are forced to interact with the space as well as each other. It may also help to put new twists on standard settings so the characters are more likely to make nuanced observations about their environment because something funny, creepy, or annoying about the space triggers an emotional response.

For instance, if you must have a scene in a restaurant, make it a speakeasy instead. And maybe it's a place where everyone inside is lurking in shadow trying to avoid being seen—or maybe a heavy metal band is playing and your viewpoint character gets caught in a mosh pit whereupon he gets in a fight which demonstrates his skills as an assassin. Or perhaps you're writing a comedy and you can create a restaurant that's part petting zoo where animals start eating from patron's plates—or maybe the spin is as simple as creating a diner where the rude waitresses zoom by on roller skates.

The point is that the environment for each scene should be more than a mere backdrop. Your readers should get a clear sense of place as determined by action plus dialogue, and the use of that space should feed the conflict and advance the storytelling. You also want to vary your setting from scene to scene instead of having the cast attend the same locals again and again.

WHITE ROOM SYNDROME

White room syndrome occurs when the sense of place and what the scene looks like is not clear based on the narrative or dialogue, but may feel obvious to you as the writer. This manifests when you have a long series of dialogue exchanges with no action beats or narrative details. It may also be a byproduct of having a grand concept that you haven't anchored to an appropriate locale. We obviously want to avoid this since the goal for both fiction and creative nonfiction is to create immersive material where the audience can visualize, empathize, and relate to the characters in the story. You also don't want to get in the habit of developing scenes that could take place anywhere. Readers crave specificity—especially if you are mining events from your life for a memoir—so work to develop setting elements that are memorable and help feed the conflict in your scene.

To do this, supplement character interactions with gestures and action beats to help the reader get a true sense of place. This can also be accomplished through the dialogue by the things each character chooses to discuss. So ask yourself: *What kind of person is my character, and what kinds of things they would observe?*

Start by giving your characters objects and other people to interact with as well as things to do so that they can move about the space. These movements can be motivated by a character's internal or external goal for the scene. A nervous eyewitness may pace the length of a sidewalk or an angry customer may pound the counter while screaming for his check. Sometimes you can even use that environment to mirror a character's emotional state *and* aggravate them at the same time so that the setting provides the impetus for the movement. For example, two characters may be engaged in an argument and one intentionally boards the wrong subway train to escape the other person who doggedly follows, and the confrontation is further amplified by the jostling of the subway car as they speed off in the wrong direction from what they both originally intended.

This puts things in motion so the audience can visualize the scene. This also prevents the interaction from feeling static. Remember, even once we know the environment, we don't want two people simply sitting in one place speaking back and forth. This is known as *talking head syndrome* and should also be avoided. But most importantly, movement gives the scene a sense of realism and breaks up the monotony of characters constantly talking.

But, be careful. We don't want to dump a bunch of setting description at the top of the scene and just expect that information to carry through. Instead, sprinkle details throughout as your characters notice more about their environment. That is to say, when you use the dialogue to focus on setting alone, it feels forced. However, if you blend the setting into the conflict or story problem, the particulars of the location help drive the scene as we saw with the Harry Potter example.

Also, consider your characters' personalities when incorporating setting into dialogue. Who is this person, and why would they notice certain things? Which of their five senses do they default to the most? Or do they rely on their sixth sense (intuition)? For example, a spy may be conscious of the number of ingresses and egresses in a location or how much the person they are interrogating is sweating. Perhaps an elderly woman may be more concerned by the bone-shattering bass of her next-door neighbor's car stereo than the questions being posed to her by her bridge partner.

On the other hand, a child might be more in tune with the smell of a location, especially if the aroma is reminiscent of her favorite cookies. Where that scent is coming from and why, can help create an emotional anchor for your dialogue as well as setting signposts that establish a sense of place for your scene. The stronger a character feels about the space, the stronger their description—and the more likely they are to continue building on that description in a significant way throughout the story. So, don't allow the need to establish an environment drive the scene. Instead, let the character's opinions, reactions, and feelings define the space.

Lastly, establish setting in advance of an important scene taking place there, especially if that scene is the climax. Have your protagonist visit earlier and foreshadow everything the reader will need to understand in order for the future moment to work. Failure to do this will ruin the pacing for that special scene because you'll need to stop every five seconds to explain the environment and how things work—when you should be gearing up for the story's peak.

Bottomline: When building dialogue that incorporates setting, ensure that you've given your characters something to do, something to react to, and somewhere to go—anchor the reader in the details of your setting through the characters' actions, reactions, and emotions. When you're choosing the setting, choose one that will complicate the purpose or add conflict to the scene. Readers want a location that challenges the protagonist either physically, emotionally, or mentally. Don't allow the audience to lose touch with the space or each character's purpose within the scene. Sprinkle elements of setting throughout the narrative and dialogue to create rich characterization and worldbuilding.

Pacing

Speech, even in written form, commands attention, so it is important that the language has a compelling pace. In literary terms, pacing is the rate of a story's forward progression. But like a roller coaster, stories have highs and lows. The dialogue may need to move faster for a homicide cop's heated argument with his partner and slower when that same detective searches the crime scene for clues. Pace is an essential part of storytelling, and writers need to be conscious about what they hope to accomplish when they make each shift.

This section covers some of the ways you can alter your dialogue to develop effective changes in pace.

In general, dialogue progresses the story much faster than narrative description alone. So if you want to increase the tempo of a scene, create a few dialogue passages where the narrator's voice is kept to a minimum. Create quick statements and pithy responses. Allow the characters to finish each other's sentences. Use language that's simple and straightforward. You could also eliminate the dialogue tags so that the conversational rhythm feels more like a tennis match. By sticking solely with the dialogue, the scene keeps its momentum and isn't slowed down by extraneous detail. This permits the reader to experience the characters' struggles without adding material that may pull the audience out of the moment.

Conversely, narrative is a great way to slow down a scene. Let's say a pair of young lovers are trying to share their feelings, but there is hesitation on both parts. The text may contain a number of commas, ellipses, or dashes to illustrate their hesitation. You could also use the narrative portions of the text to highlight their indecision and the importance of the moment through pauses, silences, gestures, or thought. Granted, internal thought is considered a type of dialogue, but it resides in the narrative as a way to reveal the characters' emotions. Scenes that explore inward feelings such as fear, doubt, anxiety, or anticipation are often slower by design. Think of them as a roller coaster slowly clicking up the peak of the hill where decision and action reside.

To slow a scene, you can also use longer sentences and paragraphs, more complicated language, or incorporate anecdotes that take longer to get to the point. Quentin Tarantino is a master at that last technique. His films often have his bad guys tell a rambling story that, initially, seems irrelevant to the current dialogue, but some larger observation or element of metaphor embedded in the story is what ultimately brings the scene to a turning point. This is beautifully demonstrated in the opening of *Inglourious Basterds* (2009) where Hans Landa (Christoph Waltz) tells a story about rats as he questions a French farmer to gain the location of some missing Jews. This longwinded non-sequitur reduces the scene's action and pace without destroying the tension—in fact, it amplifies it as the farmer and the audience wonder where things are going.

But overall, how do we keep our story from dragging? Have the external action of the plot vary in its intensity so the protagonist's interest or ability to pursue their goal waxes and wanes with the difficulty or ease of their environment. Or to put it plainly, you can always alter the pace of the story by bringing in some new challenge or emotion.

For example, perhaps your protagonist is served divorce papers just as he finds what's believed to be the key clue in the case. The life distraction may reduce his ability to concentrate on his work and pull time away from the case, making it harder to follow up on leads. Or it may have the opposite effect of allowing him to move more quickly because he no longer needs put time into his marriage. Regardless, do you see how external events and internal reaction can significantly affect the ebb and flow of the story? So, to keep your novel fresh, you can also use the plot in conjunction with the dialogue to push or pull back the pace as needed.

But how do you determine if your story is well paced? That's a more nuanced question that requires an examination of your text and its protagonist. To discover the answer, start by examining each scene for clues to determine if you need a slower or faster approach:

- What purpose does this scene serve? Is it meant to be heart-pounding or heart-warming?
- How do I see this scene fitting into the overall narrative? Is it in a position meant to induce action or reflection?

- How much dialogue, action, and narrative have I used in this scene compared to the ones around it? Have I worked to achieve a balance between scenes? Do any of them need more or less dialogue, action, or narrative to achieve a more cohesive flow?
- Does the scene feel rushed or like it is missing a beat? (Slow down.)
- Does the scene feel dull or rambling? Is it saying too much while at the same time saying nothing at all? (Speed up plus add conflict and tension.)
- Do I keep inserting my personal agenda or humor into the scene rather than allowing the characters' dialogue, action, and opinions to speak for themselves?

When determining if your story is well paced, you can also consider your genre. Thrillers, adventure fiction, and suspense typically rely on physical action over reflection, so the pace remains relatively fast. Such novels would have very few languid scenes. In fact, any slow scenes those writers choose to include would probably be strategically placed to provide the audience with an explanation or emotional break from the tension-filled story highs. On the other hand, characters in romances and cozy mysteries tend to spend more time in reflection because they are more character-driven than plot-focused. And so, their stories maintain a steadier pace with any highs and lows being tied to emotion or discovery.

But regardless of what your genre typically requires, I encourage you to learn how to regulate pace at will so that you're always in control of your story's tempo. To get you started, here's a recap of the tips covered in this chapter.

To slow down a scene that's moving too fast, consider the following techniques for reducing pace:

- Add more gesture, description, and internal dialogue.
- Write longer sentences and paragraphs.
- Use more sophisticated or complicated language (include jargon).
- Change setting. Private settings are often less hectic than public ones.
- Intersperse backstory with the dialogue or replace some dialogue with narrative.

To speed up a scene that's moving too slow, consider the following techniques for increasing pace:

- Craft shorter statements and replies. Allow characters to cut each other off.
- Use simple, straightforward language.
- Omit any words, sentences, phrases, tags, or gestures that fail to illuminate character or advance the plot.
- Use emotional shorthand rather than going through things step by step. In other words, avoid dialogue that drones on and on about a single subject. This slows the pace of your story. You don't need to give the audience every detail about a topic. Summarize. Consolidate. Condense. In fact, you can always cut to another scene and return to the same conversation but fast forwarded a few beats. This can add dimension and suspense to your tale while also breaking up a monotonous pace.

Exercise: Pacing

Exercise: Look for a scene in your manuscript that has yet to find its optimal pace. Conduct an examination of your viewpoint character to troubleshoot the issue. Is she talking too much or not enough? Is the scene focused too much on her thoughts rather than the action or vice versa? Are her interactions with the other characters significant (i.e. do they have a purpose that serves the overall narrative)?

Remember, a scene can have more than one pace, moving from fast to slow to mirror the emotions of the characters, but you as the writer must be consciously aware of when it's happening and the purpose it will serve.

Time

In fiction, it is best to compress time. You don't need to show a character's nighttime ritual when they come home from work or the protagonist's walk through the airport if nothing significant to the plot happens during that period. Use a transitional phrase, indirect dialogue, or summary speech to encapsulate the portion of time you're skipping. This will help acclimate the audience as you move from scene to scene.

> "When we started dating **three weeks ago**, you didn't have a problem with my drinking."
>
> **The next day,** I met Mary at the train station...
>
> **Two weeks passed** before he called me...
>
> "What should I do? **It's only been a month since** we started sleeping together, and now he wants me to meet his parents."

It also helps to create space on the page to separate the two sections of time so that the changeover is visually apparent as well. If the passage of time is significant, some writers use asterisks or the pound sign in the space as an additional indicator.

Foreshadowing

Foreshadowing is the act of subliminally cluing the audience into the truth about a narrative, thus, psychologically conditioning them to accept the truth by ensuring that everything they (subconsciously) see supports the final reveal. This technique is important to dialogue because it lends itself to building suspense. The audience can feel that something compelling is on the horizon even if they can't exactly pinpoint what that may be.

In this section, you will find three stellar techniques for using your dialogue to foreshadow a problem or event:

The hint: "You look tense. Maybe we shouldn't go out tonight." The appearance of these small clues is just enough to make the audience wonder why they exist or what they might mean. This approach builds tension and suspense but may require reinforcement through various forms of suggestion before the full course of events are revealed.

The blatant statement of fact: "That guy looks creepy." These are throwaway statements, observations, or actions that produce a truthful or relatively harmless result. However, this element of foreshadowing unwittingly (for the characters and audience) initiates a chain of events that are vastly more complex, challenging, or sinister.

The denial: "I'll never cheat on my wife." This is the act of tipping the scale so far in one direction that the observant reader will understand that the plot will hinge on the reversal. The trick with this approach is to ensure that even if the foreshadowing is obvious—i.e. that he *will* cheat on his wife—the road we take to get to that big reveal is vastly different from anything the audience would have imagined. In other words, deliver on your promise of the affair, but be sure to keep the audience guessing about the means and motive.

Although the names for the aforementioned categories may imply a heavy hand, the goal is subtlety. Position your foreshadowing—whether dialogue or action—during moments when it may potentially go unnoticed by the audience. Plant a subconscious seed. And of course, the earlier and the more often you foreshadow, the more likely it will be that your reader will accept and understand the truth when it is revealed.

Exposition

Writers often demonize the word *exposition* because many people have associated the term with information dumps and extraneous details. Obviously, if a fact is interesting but doesn't serve the story or drive the plot, the lines should be removed. However, exposition by definition involves the elements *needed* to set the scene, identify the characters, and establish the situation. Your job as the author is to curate the right information at the right time, and there are two main ways to deliver that data: dialogue and narrative.

Now, if you do have some exposition you want to share through dialogue, the most obvious solution is to break it into smaller chunks and spread that information over several scenes using the mouths of several characters so that it's less noticeable. To aid in this endeavor, consider all the background and history needed to tell your story in a cohesive manner. Rank the information in order of importance, and align the most important details with the appropriate portions of the text.

For example, if there is a crucial piece of backstory that involves the town's history and there's a moment in the book when the town's having a festival, that's the best time to share the information, not before. Not after. Never bog your audience down with information they don't need, and never force your characters to deviate from their goals to talk about elements of plot or backstory.

Maid-and-Butler Dialogue

As you're writing the opening chapter of your book, you may be tempted to have the characters tell each other things they already know or speak about subjects they'd normally never discuss simply for the sake of informing the audience about backstory or some technical aspect of an upcoming event. This act of two characters re-informing each other of facts that are common knowledge in their world is known as "maid-and-butler dialogue" or the "as you know" trope.

The moniker comes from the stage—certainly during Shakespeare's Elizabethan Era but perhaps even as far back as the ancient Greeks of Euripides's day—where two characters (usually low status characters such as the maid and butler) would have a gossipy conversation to inform the audience about the matters at hand. This was meant to replace the convention of starting with a chorus or narrator character who addresses the audience. Such conversations usually go something like this:

> "Hey, Mike. Do you remember how we met in graduate school during Dr. Anderson's quantum physics class?"
>
> "Absolutely, Bob. As you know, it was during that course that I came up with my initial theory for teleportation."

Putting quotes around backstory isn't dialogue. Neither character learns anything new, so there is no tension or conflict. With maid-and-butler dialogue, readers are no longer participants in your carefully crafted alternate reality; they've returned to being observers.

To be clear, maid-and-butler dialogue isn't the same as two characters mulling over clues and deciphering what they could potentially mean or reflecting on how to overcome an obstacle. Those are essential parts of any fact-finding mission and will need to happen whenever your main character discovers something that changes her view the world. Maid-and-butler dialogue is a telling technique rather than showing technique, and it almost always reads as clunky, dull language.

So if the point of the above scene is to inform the audience about Mike's superior brainpower and hint at the possibility of seeing a teleportation device later in the text, show us those ideas through behavior and interaction, not reminiscence or gossip. Fortunately, a reader's tolerance for this technique in literature is very low, forcing us to be more creative. Unfortunately, this problem is so prevalent in television and film that fiction (and creative nonfiction) writers still think it is an acceptable way to deliver exposition.

A word of warning: Film is a visual medium, so even if the characters are clearly providing super boring backstory to clarify things to come, the viewer can gain stimulus from their environment, their accents, or the way they are dressed. We do not have this luxury in literature, so we must be cleverer about how we convey data or background information.

One way to do this is to bring in a neophyte character who acts as a stand in for the audience and looks at the situation with new eyes so that his or her questions about what's to come do not feel so contrived. This person's naiveté may lend a bit of comedy to the unfolding of the information, which will keep the audience engaged and turning pages. As an example, let's consider Harry Potter. His arrival into the wizarding world as depicted in the first and second books of the series are great examples of how incorporating a novice or fish-out-of-water character can make the inclusion of backstory, the establishment of a world, or the explanation of a new concept appear seamless.

Another method is to incorporate news broadcasts or newspaper clippings that give the reader a quick overview of the problem and how it effects the larger world. And of course, if all else fails, the purest method is to sprinkle information evenly over the course of several scenes like breadcrumbs. Basically, save each specific piece of backstory for the moment when it is most relevant rather than dumping everything onto the page in one spot, giving away too much too fast. Good fiction sours when it fails to progress forward, so don't interrupt the reader with something from the past until they are clear about the present—and even then, do it briefly in a couple lines, not a couple chapters!

We must also ensure our dialogue remains as present and active as possible. An exchange that describes an off-stage event (even one in the adjacent present) doesn't have as much impact on the audience as a showing that sequence in real time. Where possible, show rather than tell. Of course, if your audience is confined to a single viewpoint, there may be some instances of telling. In those cases, infuse your dialogue with more tension by creating an urgent reason for the information exchange. Then allow the characters to fall into disagreement about the information's veracity or importance or how to proceed, et cetera. Letting the news cause conflict guarantees that both characters are active participants in the exchange and opens the door for additional characterization.

For example, a college gal named Lisa goes on the perfect date and returns to tell her roommate Jan that she's found "the one." Unimpressed, Jan wants nothing more than to return to the video game that has occupied most of her night. Lisa steps in front of the television to finish her point, causing her roommate to wipeout before reaching the game's top score. Jan, of course, blames Lisa for the loss and responds in a rage that exposes her friend's abysmal dating history. This leads Lisa to take a second, less idealistic look at her date, whereupon some suspicions are raised about her "perfect man," which act as a catalyst for the next step in the plot.

Structuring a Dialogue Scene

A well-constructed scene is essentially a mini-version of the dramatic arc (Freytag's Pyramid) that takes place over the course of the story. For instance, in each scene there is something that initiates the action in the form of an inciting incident. Complications occur, which correlates to the rising action. The scene then reaches an emotional highpoint, better known as the climax, followed by the falling action and an element that concludes the scene.

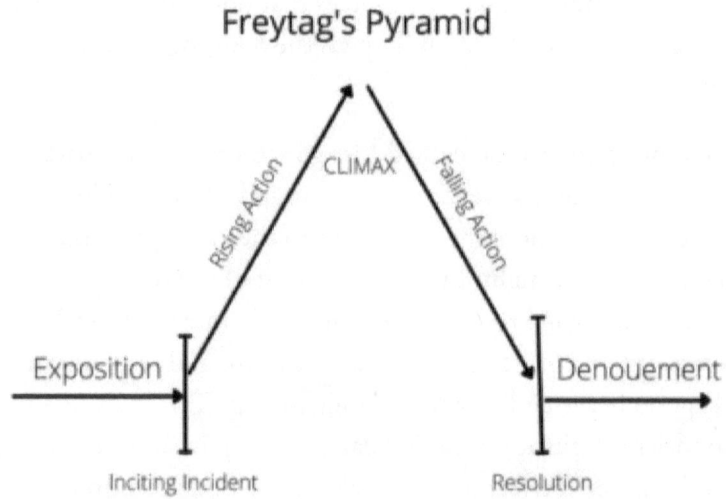

However, I'd like you to consider an alternative approach to structuring a dialogue scene. This method comes from esteemed writer Charles R. Johnson, who won the U.S. National Book Award for Fiction in 1990 for *Middle Passage*, a historical novel about the final voyage of an illegal American slave ship.

This section will give you a brief overview of Mr. Johnson's technique, but I encourage you to obtain a copy of *The Way of the Writer: Reflections on the Art and Craft of Storytelling* (2016) and read about the approach in full. The methods we will discuss can be found in Chapter 16, pages 96 to 100.

Johnson believes that we should think of our dialogue as unfolding in four stages over the course of the scene. He delineates them as entrance, rhythm, hit, and exit. They should play out in the same order every time since each serves a purpose akin Freytag's exposition, rising action, climax, falling action, and conclusion.

Let's look at them one by one:

Entrance: A proper entrance ensures that " . . . each [character] enters a scene motivated by a desire or need (or conflict) that has brought him or her there" (96).

- The entrance encompasses the opening banter that introduces the characters *(the who)* and identifies their relationship.
- Do not confuse this banter with small talk or the insignificant greetings that contribute nothing to the meaning of your scene. You must still start from a place of change or conflict so that the scene is well-paced enough to reach the scene's climax in a compelling manner.
- This is the foundation of your scene, so every piece of dialogue should have a purpose. The point of the entrance is to hint at what the scene will be about.

Rhythm: It is not until the conversation has established a flow that we get into the heart of *why* the characters have arrived at this particular place and *how* that interaction fits into the overall story.

Hit: The hit is "...that heightened moment in their exchange when the issue (or conflict) that has brought them together is finally revealed" (97).

- *What they want* or what constitutes the problem is exposed
- This problem can be a first-time revelation or the unveiling of an old wound
- The hit may not always be outwardly indicated with angry words. More often than not, it is implied. Remember, we want to avoid on-the-nose dialogue.
- This should occur during the middle or latter half of the exchange since it is considered the climax or revelatory portion of the scene. If you give away too much information at the beginning, the material has nowhere to go and the dialogue becomes anticlimactic.

Exit: The exit is the beat that concludes the scene. This does not need to be a literal departure of the participants, but it does mark the moment when the characters disengage and the narrative points toward the possibilities for the next scene.

Most exits are a reaction to the hit, so conclude the scene with a strong visual or spoken representation of the viewpoint character's feelings. Or if you prefer, this can also be a decision from that person—a decision to hide, a decision to act, a decision to back down, et cetera.

The scene should also end with a strong image or line of dialogue—something of resonance. Strong examples include a nod toward the theme or a looming threat. Just because the scene has ended doesn't mean everything needs to be tied together in a pretty little bow. Just like a heated divorce, a good scene ending should be destabilizing and leave emotional scars.

And since most scenes end in disaster, the characters should exit the scene having changed slightly. This can be a change in outlook or a change in their beliefs about the conflict. It can be a change in their approach to the story goal or a change in their feelings toward the other characters in the story. This doesn't necessarily need to be a huge life-altering change—although that's always a possibility. Maybe they simply understand something less and have grown more confused or maybe they walk away so angry that they make a rash decision. The point is that this change should help move the plot forward.

By allowing everything to culminate at the end of the scene, you create a powerful pivot for the character and the reader, who is now left to ponder how will this turn of events will affect the protagonist and his behavior in the story to come?

For a sample of a well-structured dialogue scene that uses these four phases, see the *Mission Impossible III* (2006) screenplay excerpt in the chapter on Asymmetrical Dialogue.

QUESTIONS TO ASK BEFORE WRITING DIALOGUE

As you embrace Mr. Johnson's technique and begin to understand how it can help shape your dialogue for a more compelling scene, consider the following questions. I recommend reviewing them *before* you start writing so that your entrance begins in the right place and your hit has the greatest emotional impact.

- As a writer, what do I need this scene to do? What needs to be revealed? What needs to be concealed? What should the dialogue demonstrate about the characters' personalities and current predicament? What could the audience question, expect, or anticipate about the narrative based on this exchange? How will this dialogue affect each character's goals?

- Do the characters need to speak here? If so, what do they need to learn? What events should unfold? (If you're unsure, drop the dialogue and replace it with action to test what works best.)
- Think like the characters. Consider the characters' emotions and fears: What do they want? What do they stand to gain or lose if they fail? What do they fear? What do they want to say? What would they avoid saying? What would they say instead?
- How are the characters' attitudes, emotions, and perspectives going to affect *what* they say and *how* they say it?

Abandon the literal approach to dialogue. There should be some indecision and unpredictability in the statements being made as the characters work out what it is they want to say and why.

Asymmetrical Dialogue

Asymmetrical dialogue is when a character ignores the obvious pattern of question versus answer and chooses to respond by providing a new perspective or a non-answer that generates its own set of questions or discoveries. This is meant to mimic real life where people are often lying, concealing, half-listening, misinterpreting, or talking over each other. Naturally, since our characters very rarely speak to each other with full clarity and intention, this approach acts as a wonderful way for writers to create dialogue that's intense and unpredictable.

To get started, pinpoint the main element of tension within the scene. Use humor, mocking, anger, intimidation, et cetera to cover the character's true feelings so their scene purpose lies in the subtextual realm. This transforms the conversation from a mundane exchange of information into an opportunity for each character to actively overcome obstacles and pursue their goals.

Consider this example of asymmetrical dialogue from *Mission Impossible III* (2006) – written by Alex Kurtzman, Roberto Orci, and J.J. Abrams and inspired by the 1966 TV series created by Bruce Geller. At this point in the film, Ethan Hunt has captured the reported villain, Owen Davian, and is demanding to know the secrets behind a mysterious weapon called the Rabbit's Foot. The two men, along with Hunt's partner, Luther, are sitting in the cramped cargo hold of a military airplane.

It is also important to note that, although Davian is tied up and Hunt appears to have the upper hand, the writers don't fall into the cliché of having the villain beg for mercy or divulge part of his plan. The adversaries meet each other in direct battle, neither backing down on the pursuit of their goals. In this case, Ethan wants the location of The Rabbit's Foot and Davian wants Ethan's name so that he can exact revenge.

This excerpt is from a version of the script found online labeled 1/26/06 Tan Revision.

>ETHAN
>
>You're gonna tell us everything. Every buyer you've worked with, every organization—
>
>DAVIAN
>
>What the hell's your name?
>
>ETHAN
>
>—names, contacts, inventory lists —
>
>DAVIAN
>
>Because you know what I'm gonna do next?
>
>ETHAN
>
>It's up to you how this goes.
>
>DAVIAN
>
>You have a wife? Girlfriend?

ETHAN opens the briefcase. Inside is a RED ENVELOPE.

>ETHAN
>
>You were apprehended carrying details of the location, something co-denamed 'The Rabbit's Foot.'
>
>DAVIAN

I'm gonna find her. Whoever she is, I'm gonna find her and I'm gonna hurt her. I'm gonna make her bleed and cry and call out your name, but you won't be able to do shit, you know why?

ETHAN

What's The Rabbit's Foot?

DAVIAN

Because you're gonna be this close to dead.

ETHAN

And who's the buyer?

DAVIAN

And then I'm gonna kill you right in front of her.

ETHAN

I'm gonna ask you one more time.

DAVIAN

What's your name?

ETHAN

What's The Rabbit's Foot?

DAVIAN

Who are you?

ETHAN

And who's the buyer?

> DAVIAN
>
> You have no idea what the hell's going on here, do you? You saw what I did to your little blonde friend at the factory, didn't you? That was nothing. That was fun.

ETHAN hits the table away, grabs the back of DAVIAN'S chair and drags him toward the back of the plane – he pounds a control button – the UNDERSIDE CARGO DOOR BEGINS TO OPEN – wind and noise and Davian is suddenly terrified –

> LUTHER
>
> ETHAN, STOP!

ETHAN turns DAVIAN'S chair, throwing it down into the now open door on the floor of the plane – the chair lands hard, getting jammed in the door, DAVIAN face-down and horrified – ETHAN pulls out a KNIFE:

> ETHAN
>
> WHAT'S THE RABBIT'S FOOT?!!!

ETHAN BEGINS CUTTING ALL THE STRAPS, ONE AT A TIME. THWACK! THWACK! THWACK! THWACK! Each time DAVIAN dropping—falling a little more—only a few straps left and ETHAN just keeps cutting them—

> LUTHER
>
> ETHAN, STOP!
>
> ETHAN (cont'd)
>
> Tell me what it is!!! What is it?!

One more slice and DAVIAN'S gone –

> LUTHER
>
> WE CAN USE HIM! YOU KNOW THAT! DON'T DO IT! ETHAN, DON'T!

LUTHER and ETHAN's eyes lock. The truth of what LUTHER'S saying registers.

Finally, ETHAN yanks DAVIAN back – DAVIAN slams into the floor as ETHAN hits the button – the CARGO DOOR CLOSES. Ethan sits on the floor, staring at him, all out of breath. Relatively quiet.

> LUTHER
>
> Damn, man.

DAVIAN'S breathing heavily. And ETHAN stares deep into his eyes, glaring death.

> DAVIAN
>
> What I'm selling...and who I'm selling too...is the last thing you should be concerned about. Ethan.

Notice how the conflict created by the dialogue moves the plot forward even though the two men aren't talking to each other in the standard question-and-answer pattern typical to these exchanges. Questions are being answered with questions. Statements are being repeated. Threats are being made. Sarcasm and subtext abound. Hunt is immediately rattled because Davian manages to guess his weakness—in this installment, Hunt recently married and now has a wife at home to protect.

Just as importantly, if this were a literary text, the diction and intention are strong enough to make it clear who is speaking. As fiction writers, we could remove most of the character prompts to give the scene more snap and rhythm, which the film ultimately embodies with its action and camera work. The relentless tenacity and tension built into the dialogue speaks volumes about each man's character and how far they are willing to go in pursuit of their goals.

Best of all, the scene ends on a major plot turn. Did you catch it? Hunt momentarily lets his emotions get the best of him and threatens Davian's life (a huge departure for Hunt who usually uses deception). As a result, Luther must pull Hunt back from the brink, which reveals Hunt's name and gives the villain the advantage.

But what is the benefit of having scenes that work this way? The answer is easy: Tension. Every scene, particularly those with dialogue, must have conflict and tension. Asymmetrical dialogue allows you to create disagreement, suspicion, misunderstanding, and misinterpretation quickly and easily—without necessarily resorting to physical fights and arguments. Plus, this type of dialogue sounds more realistic and can lead to some interesting character developments.

So how do we incorporate this technique into our creative writing? Here are some approaches to consider:

- **Keep each person's speech short.** Dialogue is meant to be a break from the narrative that readers can zip through easily, so don't bog the exchanges down with long speeches. But also, think about it: Rarely, do we make long speeches in real life since the listener often butts in with their own thoughts or we get distracted by our surroundings. Keep the story moving by having each person express themselves in the fewest sentences and the simplest terms.
- **Use interruptions.** Let the speakers finish each other's sentences or cut each other off. As noted earlier, this makes the dialogue feel real and helps maintain the story's pace.

- **Implement echoing, repetition, and sarcasm for clarity or conflict.**
- **Allow characters answer questions with questions.** Or better yet, have the respondent answer a completely different question—one that was perhaps implied but not yet asked. This is the heart of asymmetrical dialogue and an excellent way to develop character by having each person's dialogue focused on their personal agenda regardless of what their scene partner may need or desire.
- **Change the subject or add distractions.** Have one of the characters talk about something that seems completely off topic but has everything to do with their goals and motivation.
- **Permit the characters to address their wounds or fears rather than the current conversation.**
- **Focus the conversation on a third party.** One of the participants may decide to direct some or all of their comments to someone who isn't in the scene. These rhetorical comments are ultimately an expression of the speaker's desire, frustration, ridicule, et cetera.

Pro Tip: Despite your characters' deliberate deviations, these exchanges must serve a purpose, and the full dialogue exchange should ultimately help to advance the plot. Remember, this is not just about gimmicks and misdirection. Your job as the writer is to make sure that each line, at its core, is a cause-and-effect response to the line that comes before it and that it adequately sets up the response that follows. In essence, every line of dialogue should weave together to create a cohesive scene even though they may feel like they're meant to stand alone.

To accomplish this, you will need to understand why your characters might decline to give direct answers. Embarrassment? Distrust? Denial? Self-Doubt? Fear? Once you've figured it out, use this to determine what the character isn't saying or can't say and what they choose to express instead. To build the scene, have the characters respond to the unsaid rather than the coverup that lingers on the surface.

Now that we have some techniques under our belts, let's look at a literary example, *Murdock's Law* (1982) by Loren D. Estleman:

> His gray-blue eyes took me in swiftly from dusty crown to caked spurs. "What's your business?"
>
> "Page Murdock. I wired you last week from Helena looking for a Deane-Adams. You said you had one."
>
> "Hell of a long ride just for a gun."
>
> "I was coming anyway."
>
> His eyes narrowed. "You some kind of law?"
>
> "Does it show?"
>
> "You could be on one side or the other, from the look of you. In this business I see my share of both."
>
> "Maybe you've seen Chris Shedwell lately," I said. "My boss got a report he's on his way here. He's wanted for a mail-train robbery near Wichita two years ago."
>
> He shook his head. "Thought you boys favored those." He indicated the Army Colt in my holster. "Deane-Adams only shoots five."
>
> "I know. I used to own one."

Notice how the author doesn't muddle the pace by squeezing in unnecessary dialogue tags. We know who's speaking based on the rhythm of the scene. And even though neither man directly answers the questions posed to him, enough information is provided to keep the reader interested, drive the story, clarify motivations, and color the characterizations. The gun shop keeper is skeptical and Special U.S. Deputy Page Murdock is a cynic but neither are pushovers and both are damn good at their jobs.

In short, don't be afraid of asymmetrical conversations where your characters don't quite answer the questions posed to them. Remember, every person in a conversation should have their own agenda. And for that reason, their responses may not be completely honest or they may be seeking their own answers, thereby going against the grain of the conversation at hand. You don't want your manuscript to become a dull series of scenes where the characters say exactly what needs to be said to progress the plot. This is something to be particularly conscious about when writing crime stories since there are often investigative scenes where the viewpoint character may be asking questions as part of his quest. If everyone simply told him what he needed to hear or volunteered information without some conflict or obstacle, the dialogue would fall flat and the story would be over in ten minutes.

Besides, readers love an opportunity to read between the lines or decipher information that's intentionally misleading. That's why they turned off the television and picked up a book. This is your opportunity to get the audience involved in the action of what's being left unsaid. After all, any dialogue that draws the reader's interest is a great sign that your novel is doing its job.

Punctuating and Formatting Dialogue

Most of the frequently asked questions about dialogue involve formatting and punctuation. This section will cover what every writer needs to know about those topics so they can submit a professional looking manuscript.

WHY DO WE FORMAT DIALOGUE?

Dialogue formatting is important because it clarifies who's speaking and makes it easier for the reader to digest the text. For example, if we put the statements and reactions for each speaker in a single block paragraph, it becomes difficult to understand the scene's action.

> "Wake up," she said. "Did we miss the plane?" "Clearly you don't care about the plane or you'd be dressed." She tossed a pair of jeans onto the bed. "You got six minutes, or I'm leaving without you."

The sample that follows is much easier to read. We have line breaks to indicate changes in speaker. Dialogue tags have been modified to identify the characters to the reader.

> "Wake up," Layla said.
>
> "Did we miss the plane?"
>
> "Clearly you don't care about the plane or you'd be dressed." She tossed a pair of jeans onto the bed. "You got six minutes, or I'm leaving without you."

Now that you have a taste for why formatting is important, let's examine some of the common guidelines.

The Power of Said

Unless you're Yoda, you'd never say, "Walked I into the bathroom."

That's because we always put our subject before our verb when speaking, so it makes sense to opt for *he said* over its inverse (~~said he~~) in the majority of your writing.

In general, we want to make *said* the default speaker tag, aka dialogue attribution, for our work. After all, the purpose of a dialogue tag is to indicate who is speaking. *Said* accomplishes that simple task without drawing attention to itself.

However, some writers believe that *said* is not creative enough or that using it repeatedly can become tiresome. The truth is that the reader doesn't notice *said* the same way we don't notice there are nearly 26 uses of *the* on this page. The dialogue tag is functional fixture in literature. If you're worried *said* makes your work repetitious or dull, that's more likely a sign that your characters and conflict aren't pulling their weight. When dialogue resonates with the proper combination of action, attitude, personality, and tension, the tag becomes unnecessary.

Also, keep in mind that dialogue attributions are about verbal expression. Words like laughed, snorted, smiled, pouted, shrugged, barked, and howled aren't elements of speech. If you must select an occasional alternate to *said*—although I'd argue you could get by without them—opt for simple words like *replied, answered, shouted,* or *whispered*, which are elements that either speak to volume or verbal action.

Avoid using a dialogue tag and an action beat on the same line. One element is enough to identify the speaker.

> Weak: Tim tapped his watch and said, "Hurry up."
>
> Strong: Tim tapped his watch. "Hurry up."

Strong: Tim said, "Hurry up."

But with those basics in mind, I should point out that *said* can be overused and should be eliminated if the constant use causes the scene to lose its rhythm. In the following example, dialogue tags are being used when it isn't necessary.

"Hurry up," Tim said.

"I am going as fast as I can," Gina said. "What's your hurry?"

"Don't get snippy. I just want good seats," Tim said.

"Relax. No matter where we sit, you'll still be able to wink at the drummer," Gina said.

"What?" Tim said.

"Don't think I haven't noticed how you feel about her," Gina said.

If you have a clear rhythm of back and forth between two characters or it is absolutely clear through context who is speaking, it is okay to remove the dialogue tags to aid the scene's flow. Just be sure to include them when using three or more characters or whenever the identity of the speaker comes into question for the audience. You don't want such a small mistake frustrating your reader or breaking the illusion of your storytelling.

"Hurry up," Tim said.

"I am going as fast as I can," Gina said. "What's your hurry?"

"Don't get snippy. I just want good seats."

"Relax. No matter where we sit, you'll still be able to wink at the drummer."

"What?"

"Don't think I haven't noticed how you feel about her."

To reduce the number of dialogue tags, you can also use setting and action to solidify the context and help clarify who is speaking.

"No way, doc. I can't afford surgery."

"Calm down, Mr. Williams. It is a common procedure that takes less than an hour."

"You're in luck." Nurse Hu handed me a printout. "Your insurance covers it. See you Friday."

In this example, since the first speaker is addressing the doctor, it is safe to assume that the doctor's response follows on the second line. Notice that once a third speaker is introduced, that person's words start on a new line and are identified using an action beat that furthers the progress of the scene. Also, if this scene were longer, we'd be able to identify different speech patterns for the three speakers. The patient speaking in colloquialisms, the doctor using formalities, and the nurse talking in clipped phrases.

You can even play around with dialogue tag when you only have one speaker. Consider this example:

"Okay, cadets," **said Mrs. Phillips.** "We're going to review the Pythagorean Theorem. Anybody finish Chapter 3?"

The room filled with an uneasy silence as the four boys looked everywhere but in her direction.

> "Do we at least understand it's the relationship between the sides of a right triangle?"
>
> Billy erupted in a series of loud burps, which elicited a round of laughter from the others.
>
> "I'll take that as a 'no.' Billy, give me thirty pushups, then turn to a page 44."
>
> "You're not a ranking officer. You can't make me—"
>
> "No pushups. No grade."

Did you catch that since there was one main speaker here that only one dialogue tag was used? The identifications are made clear through context. Keep it simple.

Conversely, avoid weird tags—like *prompted, chortled, quipped, cajoled,* et cetera—that include adverbs. Words of that ilk pull focus and cause the reader to wonder more about your diction than your dialogue. Focus instead on creating clear action beats and motivations that provide clarity to your conversations. Here's an example of **weak writing** that you should avoid:

> "You need to quit it right now!" Mom bellowed with authority.
>
> "But she hit me first," I whined sullenly.
>
> "I don't care what she did," Mom continued with finality.
>
> "You suck," I angrily huffed under my breath.

Notice how the spoken words have no snap. They drag because the rhythm and pace is off. We also lose the meaning behind the interaction because we're spending all our time deciphering the dialogue tags—some of which are longer than the words spoken.

In general, the tone of the scene should be reflected through the words spoken in dialogue, not through the dialogue tags. Rather than working to get rid of said, be more diligent about using strong verbs and clear imagery in your dialogue and vivid action in your narrative.

Bottomline: Focus on your character's dialogue and worry about the tags later. Some writers eliminate tags altogether, especially when there are only two people speaking and it's easy to follow the pattern.

Adverbs: Let's Talk About Those "-ly" Words

"You can find published novels in which authors use one flashy dialogue tag after another . . . . I didn't tell you that the frequent use of such tags would prevent you from being published. I only said that they indicate that the author is an amateur or that he lacks the sensitivity to appreciate the musical qualities of language. Books full of inept dialogue tags get published all the time. Of course they do. Not all published writers are good writers."

~Dean R. Koontz in *How to Write Best Selling Fiction* (1981)

Avoid using adverbs with your dialogue tags (i.e. to modify *said*) because it amounts to telling rather than showing and deprives the reader the opportunity to make their own interpretation. Adverbs place too much emphasis on the way the dialogue is expressed thus diluting the important stuff that drives the plot—i.e. the speech and its intent.

Remember, the verb in your tag already describes the action of speaking. The adverb is merely a modifier, so eliminate the superfluous middleman and let the verb-dialogue combo do its work. If you need to further emphasize the way something is said, you probably weren't specific enough in the first place and should go back to reexamine your dialogue.

Weak: "Leave me alone," he said angrily.

Strong: He slammed his fist into the wall. "Leave me alone."

Since the character acts prior to the dialogue, the attribution isn't needed. It is clear from context how he feels, and we even gain some insight into his personality because only a hothead would punch a wall. Sure, an occasional *hastily* or *quietly* isn't going to kill the work in progress, but words like *smilingly*, *cringingly*, *heatedly*, or *laughingly* will sink it faster than the Titanic. The problem with adverb use of this kind is that they are nonsensical words that would never be used in natural speech. They are just a big distraction. You're better served using an action or narrative beat to add body language, facial expression, or movement to your dialogue instead.

If the writing is strong, the audience should be able to infer what a character is feeling through a set of actions, reactions, and subtext as provided by the author. The use of adverbs tacked onto the dialogue tag is a crutch that tells the reader how to think and feel about the situation rather than providing the context for the audience to come to that conclusion on their own.

Unconvinced? Read the first chapter of *Nabokov's Favorite Word Is Mauve: What the Numbers Reveal About the Classics, Bestsellers, and Our Own Writing* (2017) by Ben Blatt, which contains an unofficial study about "-ly" adverbs. Blatt crunches the literary numbers and argues that the most successful books use fewer of these tricky little words than the average. If you prefer, you can read a summation of his findings via the *Literary Hub* article titled "Toni Morrison is More Hemingway Than Hemingway Himself".[1]

---

1. https://lithub.com/toni-morrison-is-more-hemingway-than-hemingway-himself/

A Final Note on Adverbs

When using an adverb to modify a verb, you do not need to include a comma.

> Weak: "Stop, or I'll shoot," she said, nervously.

If you feel the adverb is needed, do not include the comma.

> Better: "Stop, or I'll shoot," she said nervously.

However, as noted throughout this chapter, it is best to avoid the adverb altogether and opt for an action beat or narrative element.

> Best: "Stop, or I'll shoot!" Her voice trembled.

Present Participles

A present participle is an *-ing* verb used as an adjective to describe an action. When we use present participles in dialogue tags, it sometimes helps to paint a more vivid picture. However, as with adverbs, writers tend to go overboard, not realizing that they are often better served by using full-sentence action beats that contain active verbs. Present participles can sometimes morph into convoluted fragments where it's unclear who took the action or when they took the action. Consider the examples below to get a better understanding of how the technique can become a pitfall.

> Incorrect: **Skipping across the courtyard.** "Recess! Hooray!"

> Incorrect: **Galloping beside the river, enjoying the sunset.**

In these examples, the narrative portions do not qualify as complete sentences because they lack a subject. Remember, in this case *skipping* and *galloping* are present participles, not verbs. Plus, they are confusing. Who is skipping and galloping? Do not leave the reader hanging.

> Better: Galloping beside the river on her steed, Mariah enjoyed the sunset.

> Better: Entering the field, Raj tripped and fell flat on his face.

These examples are much better because they are grammatically correct. We have a clear subject (Mariah / Raj) and verb (enjoyed / tripped). The section with the present participle is just an added bit for clarity. However, I still don't recommend this structure because it puts the subject after an action and blends a series of events together. Three things happen to the character in the second sentence, yet the writer doesn't take time to clarify them in a compelling manner. Why was Raj entering the field? What caused him to trip? Did he realize anything when he hit the ground? This seems like an important moment that the audience would want to fully experience and better understand. You're a writer. Don't be afraid to write. Get descriptive and structure your sentences so that each action, cause, and effect are clear.

> Best: Raj entered the Cougars football arena for his first home game. When his name was announced, he stepped up to the 50-yard line and waved at the crowd. But it wasn't long before his knees gave way and his nerves took over. Face plant... in front of the entire school... including Lisa, who was his whole reason for joining the team.

Obviously, this isn't as concise as the present participle example, but it is far more interesting to read and gives your audience greater insight into how things unfold.

Another present participle element that often sinks the narrative is the habit of using more than one beat per sentence.

> Reaching for my hand, she giggled. "You're such a cutie pie," she said, batting her lashes.

Double particle action slows the pace, dilutes meaning, lacks concision, and confuses the order of action. For instance, in the sentence above. Is she giggling while reaching or after? And why is she giggling? Is it because she had to reach for his hand or because maybe her hand is clammy because she's nervous. Many of the same questions apply to the back half of the sentence. Is she batting her lashes during or after the statement? Not to mention, that with so many things happening at once, the dialogue is buried. In this instance, it may have been better to simply start with some narrative or direct thought to clarify how she feels then introduce the dialogue so the reader can focus on one thing at a time.

Bottomline: Using present participles within the dialogue attribution can aid in creating an action beat. However, active verbs often have a stronger impact.

And of course, writers should avoid using adverbs and the present participle together:

> Weak: Running quickly across the lawn, Mom waved her arms to get my attention. "Honey, you forgot your lunch."

> Strong: I turned to find my mother sprinting toward me, arms flailing.
>
> "Honey, you forgot your lunch."

> Weak: Shouting loudly over the radio, Jane leaned over and asked, "Do you love me?"
>
> Strong: Jane leaned over and raised her voice above the music. "Do you still love me?"

Again, the adverb is redundant and doesn't add anything new to clarify meaning or inflection. In both instances, the rewrite provides clarity and concision. Even though we're using present participles, it's clear who's doing the action and the order of those events makes logical sense. Do whatever you can to make it easy for your audience to envision the scene.

A FINAL NOTE ON PRESENT PARTICIPLES

If you must use a present participle to modify a verb, you need to include a comma as noted in all of the examples in this section. However, it is often better to write the sentence with an active verb to create a sentence that can standalone as its own beat.

> Weak: "You're such a cutie pie," she said, batting her lashes.
>
> Strong: "You're such a cutie pie." She batted her lashes.

Dialogue: Formatting Guidelines

Although there aren't any specific rules about where to add your dialogue attributions. The common approach is to insert the tag at the first natural pause in the spoken sentence. This helps to identify the speaker at the earliest moment possible and incorporates the tag without disrupting the flow of the dialogue. This section will show you how to format the placement of your dialogue attributions and provide rules for punctuation.

Use double quotation marks to denote words spoken aloud. Think of the quotation marks as an amplifier. The first set of quotation marks highlights what's being spoken aloud while the second set is important because it closes or ends the concept of what's being spoken.

"Help!" Max shouted.

"Hey, man," said Mark. "Wait up!"

Anastasia asked, "Is there room for one more?"

"I don't know where they went," Rick replied.

Study the examples. Notice that the verb used in each dialogue tag remains lower case regardless of the position it takes in the sentence. This occurs because the attribution is the continuation of the dialogue sentence (even if that dialogue ends in a question mark or exclamation point).

Incorrect: "Have you washed the dishes?" She asked.

Correct: "Have you washed the dishes?" she asked.

Correct: "You washed the dishes!" she said.

Use commas to denote the speaker tag. If the speaker tag appears at the beginning of the sentence, it is immediately followed by a comma. If the tag appears at the end of the sentence, it is preceded by a comma that's placed inside the quotation marks. The tag is then followed by a period.

Allison said, "I'll show you mine if you show me yours."

Allison asked, "Can you show me yours?"

"Let's get ready for some Jenga," Crystal said.

"Let's get ready for some Jenga," she said.

If the dialogue tag breaks a single sentence into two parts, it is punctuated with flanking commas. The comma in front of the tag goes inside the quotes and the comma rear comma is outside of the quotation marks flush with the tag.

"If I won the lottery," Emma said, "I'd love to visit Madrid."

If the tag falls between two independent sentences, punctuate the tag in the front with a comma that goes inside the quotation marks. Punctuate it on the back end with a period to denote the end of the sentence.

"I just won the lottery," Emma said. "I'd love to visit Madrid."

Use tags and beats sparingly. We typically only use one attribution or action beat when the character's speech is less than three lines. **Avoid the following:**

Incorrect: "Well," Tommy said, "I have no idea where I want to go for dinner." He scratched his head. "Is there a gluten free place nearby?" he pondered. "Maybe we should just order in." He shook his head in dismay.

Use a new paragraph to indicate a new speaker, even if that response is a single word or short phrase. Every time someone new speaks or the dialogue changes speaker, start a new line. This will help make it clear who's speaking.

"Hurry, Tanita." The words tumbled out of me fast as fire. "The ice cream truck is coming."

"Who gave you money?"

"Ma."

"No way."

Capitalize the first word if it starts a full sentence of dialogue.

"You need to leave," Rita said. "I'm late for work."

Laura said, "These dishes are dirty."

"Do you need a wake-up call?" Mary asked.

Here are two examples of sentences that have been split down the middle, so this capitalization rule doesn't apply to the second part of the dialogue. Notice how the tag is placed in the natural pause point for the sentence (between the dependent and independent clauses).

"If you eat your veggies," Matt said, "we can all go for ice cream."

"Unless it's fish," Kamilah said, "my kids won't eat it."

Question marks and exclamation points. If you add a tag after a line of dialogue that's a question or exclamation, the pronoun should not be capitalized.

"May I have my own ice cream cone?" she asked.

"May I have my own ice cream!" she said.

Abby asked, "May I have my own ice cream cone?"

Abby said, "May I have my own ice cream!"

Notice that because the question marks and exclamation points are part of the statement being spoken aloud, those terminal pieces of punctuation remain inside the quotation marks regardless of their position in the sentence. Periods also remain inside the quotation marks but only if they act as closing punctuation.

"Sorry. I don't have any money to buy ice cream," said Pearl.

"Sorry," said Pearl. "I don't have any money to buy ice cream."

Devonte said, "They are all out of ice cream."

Decide on the correct punctuation for the end of your dialogue sentences, and determine if it should go inside the quotation marks. Be advised: There should only be one piece of end punctuation. To complete this task, you will need to consider the relationship between the dialogue and the narrative parts since the punctuation is based on their interconnectivity.

Double v. Single Quotes. If a speaking character quotes another person (or some other material) within her dialogue, use single quotes for the quotation.

"When you said, 'I stole the Maltese Falcon,' did you mean it?"

She said, "The first words out of his mouth were 'no deal,' and things just got worse from there."

"The first words out of his mouth were 'no deal,'" she said.

Look closely at the final portion of the second example. Note that the comma (like the period in the previous example) falls inside the quotes.

In addition, the second example correctly uses three quotation marks at the end—one single quotation for the quote within a quote, 'no deal,' and a double quotation mark to indicate the end of the spoken dialogue.

Reprinting songs or poems. If you want to represent a song or poem in your work, you will need to separate the verse or verses from the main text with a space and center the material on the page. To illustrate, here is the first stanza of "Still I Rise" by Maya Angelou, an American poet and activist:

> You may write me down in history
>
> With your bitter, twisted lies,
>
> You may trod me in the very dirt
>
> But still, like dust, I'll rise.

Punctuate long speeches with care. When one character makes a long speech, and you want to break up the paragraphs, the proper punctuation is to put a quotation mark at the start of the first paragraph and each new paragraph break but not at the end of the paragraphs contained within the quotation. The close quote should only occur after the final line of the speech. Study this short example:

> "I can't do this anymore, Steve. I am tired of sneaking off to the bathroom every time you're feeling frisky. I want more. Dinner. Dancing. A real date with someone who is proud to be seen with me.
>
> "But the truth is you're engaged—don't bother denying it. I found out the truth this morning, and I'm not interested in playing the fool another minute. Either break off the engagement or never see me again."

You will find this method in most English textbooks, but for creative writing the approach lends itself to looking like a typographical error. Contemporary writers typically prefer to create breaks through action or reaction. Compare this to the previous example to note the difference in punctuation.

> "I can't do this anymore, Steve. I am tired of sneaking off to the bathroom every time you're feeling frisky. I want more. Dinner. Dancing. A real date with someone who is proud to be seen with me."
>
> I shifted my weight from foot to foot, hoping it would strengthen my resolve.
>
> "But more importantly, I know you're engaged—don't bother denying it. I found out the truth this morning, and I'm not interested in playing the fool another minute. Either break off the engagement or never see me again."

Group Conversation of Three or More Speakers. You will need to update the tags anytime a new speaker is introduced or whenever it is unclear from context who might be speaking. Don't worry about the possible obtrusiveness of the dialogue tags. Readers will be grateful that they won't need to do any mental math to determine the speaker. However, if you feel the scene is too busy, you may want to ask yourself if all of the characters are needed for the scene. It may be possible that your story is better served if two of the characters are cut to allow them to have a separate conversation about the outcome of the group scene later in the book. This offers opportunities for secrets, deception, and alliances to form.

Another helpful practice for creating group conversations is to create a clear activity or specific position within the environment for each character so the audience has an easier time keeping track of everyone's movement and purpose. If it helps, picture the scene like a stage play and place your characters strategically within the setting. You can also have the protagonist act as an orchestrator or mediator for the event where all of these characters arrive for discussion. That way, you have a person acting as a stopgap to regulate speaker frequency. Focus on a couple characters at a time rather than trying to juggle everyone.

For scenes involving a crowd or community, don't feel like you need to have names for every character. It is fine to simply address a couple people by their attire, especially if they'll never be heard from in the narrative again.

Action beats stay outside the quotation marks. These beats are meant to indicate what a character is doing as they speak, so for clarity, they must remain on the same line as the speaker's words. Do not put a speaker's action in a separate paragraph. Write the beat so the context is clear, and punctuate it as its own sentence that's separate from the dialogue.

Sam cocked the gun. "Put your hands up."

Margo pounded her shot glass down on the bar then laughed. "You got that right!"

Linda's eyes filled with tears. "I hate you."

"You finally washed the dishes!" She stared at the sink in disbelief.

In each example, notice the sentence prior to the dialogue ends with a period. Since it is an action beat, not a dialogue tag, each action sentence starts with a capital letter and receives a piece of terminal punctuation. That's how we should indicate all action even if the sentence is short.

Incorrect: "He's going to divorce her," she smiled.

Incorrect: "I won the lottery," he whooped.

Correct: "He's going to divorce her." She smiled at the news.

Correct: "I won the lottery." He whooped.

Use narrative beats. In addition to action beats, there are narrative beats containing description that can clarify the scene's imagery, intensify a moment, or develop an emotion. This is also a wonderful way to insert elements that speak to the moment through the five senses. These beats should be written as complete sentence and take terminal punctuation.

"You need to go." **Rita's hands trembled as she opened the door.** "I'm late for work."

You may also want to vary this technique by using thought beats to show a character's concerns, and/or opinions.

"Keep your distance." **Jim's tone was even, but he loathed being near her.** "I am not feeling well today."

DIALOGUE TAG PLACEMENT

You can place speaker tags before, after, or in the middle of the dialogue. The location you choose is often dependent on the action of the scene, the dialogue's location in the book, and preference. For example, it may help to start with a tag or place it in the middle of a sentence if you're opening a chapter with dialogue. This provides immediate audience clarity. Or perhaps, you want to create a snappy scene that moves quickly. Switching up the location of dialogue tags (or dropping them altogether) can increase or decrease pace, so be sure to study these rules.

Yes, of course, you can stick with just one position if that's your preference. There isn't anything grammatically wrong with that decision. Just keep in mind that writers often vary their syntax (i.e. sentence structure) to ensure readers don't get bored. Dialogue tag placement is an excellent way to do that without struggling with much tougher English rules like compound-complex sentences.

First, let's review those placement rules in case you missed them in the previous section.

If you place the tag before the sentence, the comma should go outside the quotes.

> Before: Jim said, "Keep your distance. I am not feeling well today."

If you place the tag after the sentence, the comma should go inside the quotes.

> After: "Keep your distance. I am not feeling well today," Jim said.

If you place the tag in the middle of a sentence that continues, commas should flank the tag. However, the first one goes inside the quotes and the second one remains on the outside.

> Middle: "Take those dishes," Laura said, "and put them in the sink."

However, in most instances, you won't need to split a single sentence to insert a dialogue tag. Most attributions will simply fall between two independent sentences. In which case, the punctuation would default to the after rule.

Middle: "Keep your distance," Jim said. "I am not feeling well today."

Overall, it is good to get into the practice of indicating the speaker at the first natural moment of pause as indicated by breath, so look for commas, periods, exclamation points, or interjections as way to guide your work. If there's a moment when the character stops to think or stumbles over his words, those are ideal places to add a tag. The goal is to incorporate the attribution without disrupting the musicality of the dialogue. If the sentence has more than one break point, decide what portion of the sentence you want to emphasize. Placing the tag at the beginning is good for reader clarity but often feels like taking a breath before telling a long story. A tag that falls in the middle feels like a fulcrum, propping up one idea that the rest of the sentence will explain. Tags that fall at the end tend to place a spotlight the entire sentence.

Be advised: If you are an established author, your editor will help you make these decisions based on the style guide used by your publisher. A style guide is the set of formatting and design guidelines used to create a uniform standard for publication. Common style guides include *The Chicago Manual of Style* (CMoS), *The MLA Handbook* (Modern Languages Association), and *The Associated Press Stylebook* (AP).

Exercise: Dialogue Formatting

Review the dialogue rules on formatting and punctuation.

Write a short story of at least ten sentences using mainly dialogue. Demonstrate that you understand the concepts outlined in the lesson by including the following:

- At least one sentence with the tag in front: *Bob said, "Do you like milk?"*
- At least one sentence with the tag in the middle: *"After*

dinner," Susy replied, "milk and Oreos always sound good."
- At least one sentence with an end tag: *"Interesting,"* Bob said.

Your story doesn't need to be clever or shocking, but it should have a beginning, middle, and end that make logical sense.

Action Beats

An action beat give a visual interpretation of what movement happens in the scene or where the characters exist within the space. These beats can also be internal narrative or thought. They are included in the same paragraph as the speaker's dialogue and help to provide context to the scene. Action beats can convey setting, establish character, clarify motivation or intent, and add much-needed emotion to an otherwise dull scene.

> "Keep your distance." **Jim shooed her from his bedside.** "I am not feeling well today."

Don't use action beats in place of all your dialogue tags because that can also become repetitive and cumbersome. They need to have some inherent characterization or reason for existing. If you use them constantly without purpose, then it has the opposite effect. Readers begin to wonder why some many little things are happening and what ultimate result they are having on the scene.

Action beats should weave seamlessly with the dialogue and emerge organically from what's happening. Strong action beats are able to do one or more of the following:

- Create a sense of place and movement
- Vary the rhythm and pace of the dialogue
- Enhance subtext by reflecting a character's true feelings
- Heighten tension

- Comment upon the scene question

Study this list. You do not want to fall into the trap of believing that action beats are merely pauses in the dialogue or empty gestures. They are meant to deepen your story's emotional content.

Italics, Dashes, Ellipses, and Hyphens

In this section, we will discuss the purpose and proper usage for italics, exclamation marks, and semicolons. The sections on dashes, ellipses, and hyphens will follow.

Italics

In creative writing, italics serve two purposes:

- Indicate a character's direct inner thoughts
- Draw attention to a word through emphasis

As noted in the section on internal dialogue, many professional editors are moving away from using italics to specify a character's thoughts. However, if this is something you still do, don't worry. Stylistically, it's permissible. However, too many italics can clutter the page, and they really aren't necessary since internal thought is technically part of the narrative.

However, if your character is thinking about something another character has said, put that information in italics. For example:

> He considered what his mother said to him earlier. *If you love someone, don't be afraid to set them free.* Maybe she was right.

Notice how the only portion in italics is his recollection of his mother's advice. His direct inner thoughts, i.e. the last sentence, are expressed in plain text.

Now, let's move forward and look at a few examples of italics used for emphasis. You may want to do this to help the reader understand how the character is speaking the sentence. Apply this technique sparingly because it will lose its effectiveness if applied to every line.

"We *need* your help. It's life or death."

"*Stop it!*" said Margo.

Also, don't confuse the use of italics with the use of capital letters.

Emphasis: "I'm not talking about *him*. I'm talking about *her*."

Volume & Urgency: "HELP! I'M LOCKED INSIDE."

Notice the difference? Italics imply emphasis while a fully capitalized word usually indicates a character growing in volume or a situation increasing in importance. Again, we want to use both techniques sparingly. Don't have a whole page, or even a whole paragraph, with italics or caps.

You can also use italics if you have words that need to be set apart from the rest of the narrative, like the recreation of a letter, news article, or dairy entry. In general, I would advise against this or recommend that you keep those passages short. Italics can become difficult to read over long passages and big blocks of slanted letters may annoy your reader.

Instead, if you have a long passage of internal thought or perhaps a flashback, ditch the italics. Simply start with a transition so the reader knows you're shifting away from the present narrative. After that, move forward with plain text.

As I watched my ex-wife walk away, my mind drifted to that fateful night . . .

Similarly, avoid putting prologue, epilogue, or backstory in italics. It is hard to read and serves no clear purpose.

In academic writing, italics are used to denote the titles of long works of art such as newspapers, books, plays, films, websites, television series, albums, et cetera.

> My favorite track from Prince's 1984 album *Purple Rain* is the fast-paced love song, "I Would Die 4 U."

Conversely, short works of art like articles, poems, television episode titles, and song titles are enclosed in double quotes.

Another academic use for italics involves discussing a specific term. In such instances, you can use italics to inform the reader that you are utilizing the word as part of your example, not using it in its normal form.

> Unbeknownst to most people, the term *parody* derives from the Greek word for "burlesque song or poem."

Lastly, there is a longstanding usage rule for English writing which states that foreign words should be italicized to avoid confusing them with the English ones. However, the creative writing community has recently abandoned this rule because to italicize foreign words sets them apart as "the other," which could be deemed offensive. Therefore, the prevailing practice in the publishing world is that all words should be in plain text to give them equal weight and uniformity, but you're welcome to use your own judgment on this.

Personally, I think the explanation is much simpler. Most modern stories have a diverse cast and a diverse readership, so who is to say what's foreign to your audience and what's not? Plus, it doesn't make sense to italicize, say, the occasional Korean words from a character's grandfather if most of the novel's cast is Korean. Those words wouldn't be considered foreign to them and to italicize them, even though the story is told in English, would ring false.

Again, weigh your options, and do what's best for your story.

Exclamation Marks

Thanks to text messaging, the exclamation mark has become pervasive. How many times have you received content like this:

> Did you see that?!! WTF!!!! Such a clutz!

While this is an acceptable way to punctuate a casual text, the overuse tends to annoy the fiction reader. Imagine three hundred pages of that. After a while, it just becomes clutter. Not to mention, it becomes a crutch for you as a writer. Rather than working to create genuine emotion through imagery, metaphor, and action, you're hoping to manufacture those effects through a vague reference to feeling.

Hollywood journalist Sheilah Graham drove this point home when she noted in her 1958 memoir, *Beloved Infidel*, that F. Scott Fitzgerald said this about her writing: "Cut out all these exclamation points. An exclamation point is like laughing at your own joke." Instead, use strong verbs to convey the desired emotion. Find words that enlighten the senses and infer movement or rhythm. If the words require further emphasis, clarify the action.

Bottomline: Exclamation points are a way to provide emphasis, anger, or good cheer, but don't overdo it. Too many tend to make the manuscript look amateurish. Use them strategically, not as a throwaway or an adornment. We don't want sincerity to turn comic or become an annoyance. After all, your word choice should provide enough context that exclamation points aren't necessary.

SEMICOLONS

Semicolons are used to connect closely related independent clauses. They work fine in narrative text; however (see what I just did there), it is best to avoid them in dialogue since they can easily be replaced with periods or commas. Plus, they are just another barrier for the reader since many people don't understand their use and therefore find them distracting.

Or to put it another way, we should avoid semi-colons in dialogue because they break up the narrative in a way that leaves the reader confused about where to pause for the breath and where to place the vocal emphasis of the sentence. The dialogue will appear more realistic to your audience if you limit the punctuation to commas, periods, ellipses, questions marks, em dashes, and the occasional exclamation point. That's plenty.

QUESTION MARK

In creative writing, the question mark suggests an upward inflection at the end of a sentence, not necessarily a question. So, you can use this piece of punctuation to show confusion or concern, depending on context. Also, unless you're portraying text speech in your manuscript, avoid double or triple quotation marks in your dialogue.

Avoid: "Where have you been?!?!"

Dashes: A Formal Introduction

The dash is that horizontal line that's wedged between words in a line of text. Do not confuse this with the underscore, which is the line that floats at the bottom as the name implies. A dash is longer than a hyphen and can be used to indicate a range or an interruption. Dashes are also used to separate groups of words.

Dashes come in three forms: em dash, en dash, and the double hyphen. Microsoft Word will automatically turn two hyphens into an em dash if you don't leave space before or after them.

Typesetters and fussy English teachers are often noted as saying that the en dash spans the width of the letter "N" and the em dash the width of the letter "M." Admittedly, this is difficult to gage on a computer screen, so simply keep in mind that an en dash is shorter than an em dash and that writers use the longer one (em dash) to punctuate dialogue.

EM DASH: THE DISRUPTER

Em dash. An em dash is great to use when you need a pause that goes beyond the brevity of a comma but isn't as substantial as the full stop implied by a period. They are also useful if you want to add emphasis or because the conversation and action get interrupted. Allowing characters to interrupt each other is a prime technique for controlling the pace and gaining a clear grasp on the tempo of your scene is going to help your overall story speed. It also helps your characterizations as well because you'll need to decide what kind of person would do a lot of interrupting (a boss or controlling spouse) as well as what situation would warrant such interruptions (anger or fear when trying to diffuse a bomb).

With that said, how much is too much? Well, as noted above, that will depend on the situation. Arguments lend themselves to interruptions; however, if the reason for the em dash is unclear to the audience or its use dilutes meaning, then you may want to step back from the technique.

Writing good dialogue is about focusing on the content of the scene—what is the root of the scene, what needs to be revealed, what needs to be concealed, who needs what, and what goals are they working toward both externally and internally.

Here are some formal rules to consider:

Em dashes are used to identify parenthetical information. Using em dashes instead of parentheses provides emphasis, whereas information inside parentheses often goes overlooked.

> Give your hero a worthy opponent whose intellect, talents, and strength matches—if not, surpasses—the attributes given to your hero.

Em dashes can be used to indicate a sudden change in thought on the part of a single character.

> "Could you please—oh, forget it."

> "I can't find my—wait, there it is."

Em dashes can also be used when one person interrupts another. This is the most important em dash rule for writers, especially when creating dialogue for characters who argue, talk over each other, or engage in conversations where their ideas are constantly being shut down.

Notice how there isn't any additional punctuation or attribution following the em dash except the close quote. If you need to clarify who is speaking, put the dialogue tag or action beat prior to the line of dialogue.

> "Turn left here." Gary pointed. "Left. Left. I said—"

> "I heard you." Marcie turned up the radio. "I'm not deaf. I'm just tired of your squawking. You asked me to drive, so let—"

"And you asked me to navigate, so let me navigate. Because if you'd been listening, we'd be there by now."

These are great uses of an em dash because it helps to illustrate Gary's growing frustration. We don't need any intrusive description from the narrative because we can easily infer from Gary's repetition, clipped sentences, and interruptions (as shown by the em dash) that he's doing his best to control his anger. If an actor read the material aloud, he would know to give the dialogue an irritated edge.

EN DASH: THE HELPER

As noted earlier, en dashes are shorter than em dashes and their function is less important to our conversation on dialogue. However, we will discuss one rule that may prove helpful.

The en dash is primarily used to denote a span of time or number range. Consider it the punctuation equivalent of *to* or *through*.

Read pages 11–29 for tonight's homework.

The sign says the store is open 12–5 p.m.

The 2020–2022 lockdown was the worst time of my life.

However, there are exceptions. If a number or date range is introduced with *from* or *between*, the words *to* or *through* should be used to keep the construction parallel.

My dog weighed between 30 and 45 pounds.

She was part of our family from 2009 to 2018.

Hyphen

The hyphen can be found on your keyboard, usually near the upper right, after the zero on the number bar. Hyphens are used to connect words and word parts, but they should not be confused with the dashes discussed earlier in this text. Visually, hyphens are much shorter than an en or em dash.

There are some words that are always hyphenated like editor-in-chief or mother-in-law. Hyphens are also used with prefixes like cross-examination, quasi-public, all-powerful, ex-husband, self-conscious, et cetera. This is where the dictionary becomes your best friend.

In addition, when numbers from twenty-one to ninety-nine are spelled out, they should be hyphenated.

> Thirty-six, twenty-four, and seventy-seven are my favorite numbers.

As writers, the most important rule to remember is that hyphens are the identifying marker for compound modifiers that **precede the word being modified**. A compound modifier consists of two or more words that work together to function like an adjective describing a noun. The hyphen shows readers that the words are working together as a unit of meaning.

> His rock-hard **abs** rippled through his shirt.

> A well-known **artist** created that painting.

> I hate sleeping on this be because it is rock hard.

> That artist is well known.

Avoid using a hyphen when the modifier is an adverb ending in "-ly" and an adjective.

> Incorrect: Ms. Johnson's classroom was like a heavily-guarded prison.

> Correct: Ms. Johnson's classroom was like a heavily guarded prison.

You also don't want to employ a hyphen if the words are commonly used together. For example, you wouldn't use a hyphen to denote a "fast food restaurant" or a "high school student."

Ellipses

An ellipsis consists of three periods (. . .), indicating an omission. Per *The Chicago Manual of Style* (CMOS), the periods should be separated by a single space, except when adjacent to a quotation mark—whereupon, there should be no space. Your publisher may follow a different format, but the CMOS is always a great resource if you're unsure.

In formal writing, an ellipsis indicates that words have been edited out of a direct quote, indicating the passage has been altered (most likely for concision). In creative nonfiction or commercial fiction, an ellipsis is used to represent a character lost in thought or trailing off. This concept is open to interpretation as your character may have forgotten their point or decided certain things were better left unsaid or, perhaps, they are simply hesitant about their position.

> Weak: "I don't think . . ." ~~She allowed her voice to trail away.~~ "Aw, what the heck!"

> Strong: "I wonder if . . . Never mind. It's probably not worth it."

Remember, the ellipsis informs the reader that the character's dialogue has faded away on its own. You don't need to reinforce the idea. Fill the space with a more informative action beat or continue with new dialogue.

You can also use ellipses to indicate when things are difficult to say or convey. If there's a truth that your protagonist can't face, have them stop talking. Make their scene partner work to pull the information out of them. That will ensure that all the interruptions, trailing off, and avoidance tactics we've been discussing will come to fruition. Consider this example from *A Visit from the Good Squad* (2010) by Jennifer Egan:

> Her arms had a lovely tan, although a scatter of raw pink patches marred the skin above one wrist. Scars. Dolly stared at them. "Kitty, are those . . ." she faltered. "On your arms, are they . . . ?"
>
> "Burns," Kitty said. "I made them myself."

This is a helpful tool for authors because it can also represent silence—be it comfortable, awkward, or full of tension. Additionally, the ellipsis is sometimes used in a moment of anticipation, like prior to a big reveal. The goal is to build suspense and tension.

> Another violent knock ricocheted through the door. I slowly turned the knob and peeked through crack . . . to find . . . a portly old woman with blue hair.
>
> "Donna Westlake?" she asked.
>
> "Yes . . ."
>
> "You've been served."

It should also be noted that when an ellipsis falls at the end of a complete sentence, it's usually meant as a dramatic device to imply more to come. When you use this approach, you're engaging the reader's curiosity and generating anticipation by daring them to imagine what will happen next. This is an excellent technique for signaling a cliffhanger or plot twist.

Just remember that when an ellipsis occurs at the end of a sentence, you need to add a fourth dot to represent the period.... Just be mindful of the spacing. And like the exclamation point, don't overuse ellipses.

I probably overlooked some concepts, but this book isn't a grammar text. This section is simply meant to give you the basic rules that will help you look like an intelligent writer and make your dialogue easy to follow.

RESOURCES FOR GRAMMAR AND PUNCTUATION

If you'd like more information about the rules of grammar and punctuation, invest in one of the books below. This list also includes the web addresses for two popular style guides that offer online advice about mechanics and formatting.

- *The Chicago Manual of Style Online** – https://www.chicagomanualofstyle.org/home.html
- *Writing Fiction: A Guide to Narrative Craft* by Janet Burroway, Elizabeth Stuckey-French, and Ned Stuckey-French
- *The Chicago Guide to Copyediting Fiction* by Amy J. Schneider
- *The Chicago Guide to Grammar, Usage, and Punctuation* by Bryan A. Garner
- *Garner's Modern English Usage* by Bryan A. Garner
- *AP Stylebook Online** – https://www.apstylebook.com/
- *The Perdue Online Writing Lab* – https://owl.purdue.edu/

HOW TO CRAFT KILLER DIALOGUE 201

*Some portions may require registration and/or a paid membership

STYLE GUIDES BY CATEGORY

If you're a freelance writer, it may be helpful to become familiar with the different style guides available. As with most publications, the managing editor typically has an in-house guide, but it is always helpful to know where to look when faced with writing about a new topic.

- Fiction, Nonfiction, History – *The Chicago Manual of Style*
- Journalism/News/Magazines/Web Publications – *The Associated Press Stylebook* (AP Style)
- Humanities – *The MLA Handbook* (Modern Language Association)
- Social Sciences and Behavior Manuals – *Publication Manual of the American Psychological Association* (APA)
- Medicine – *American Medical Association Manual of Style* (AMA)
- Business – *Gregg Reference Manual*
- Government – *Government Printing Office Style Manual* (GPO)

I'm Stuck! What Should I Do?

In the chapter on Structuring a Dialogue Scene, I list several questions to consider when preparing to write. However, those questions may only prove helpful if you already have a premise or plot outline from which to build your ideas.

In this section, you will find an approach to brainstorming through dialogue. If you're a plotter, you can use this checklist to create an outline. And if you're a pantser, you can use these steps to start writing.

Step 1: Find an opening line of dialogue. This can be a line from your favorite commercial or something you overheard on the street.

Step 2: Brainstorm several situations that could develop from that line. Don't use the same setting or speaker. Try to find a new location and a new context for the words. Once you do, layer in new description.

Step 3: Based on the brainstorm from the previous step, select the most contentious situation. Imagine at least two characters who occupy that space.

Step 4: Create a dialogue exchange based on the initial line of dialogue. Visualize the scene in your mind like a film, and work to hear the character talk. Have their interaction help you decide the following:

- Who is your viewpoint character? (This is usually the person with the most at stake.)
- What tense will I use to tell my story?

You don't need to know where the scene is going while you're writing it (or worry about every single rule), that's why we revise.

Step 5: Flesh out your characters. Craft character profiles or interview your heroines to create speech profiles so that you understand how everyone speaks. What do these people want? How do they sound? What motivates them toward their goals? What are they willing to sacrifice? What do they stand to lose if they fail (and gain if they win)? What will they say or do to get it?

Step 6: List several problems your characters can face on the way to their goals. What unforeseen dilemmas, choices, or conundrums can you give these characters to further complicate your story? Look for situations that create conflict and tension.

- Decide which of those elements could stand alone as scenes.
- Use Freytag's Pyramid or Charles R. Johnson's beats as well as your characters' goals and motivations to organize a series of scenes.

Step 7: How could the problems resolve? Avoid the easiest solution. What does your character need to go through to achieve a resolution to their primary conflict?

Step 8: Layer sensory details and descriptive elements over the dialogue you've created to devise a more compelling scene.

When you're sure you have the makings of a cohesive story with a suitable problem to overcome and a clear beginning, middle, and end, start writing.

Write at the same time each day to create consistency and to train your brain to provide inspiration at the moments when you need it most. Strive for two to three pages a day (about 700 to 900 words). Don't worry about editing yourself on the initial draft. You don't want to become critical of yourself early in the process because you might talk yourself out of finishing. Allowing the words to flow will help you connect with your unconscious genius or the infinite intelligence or the creative oversoul—all the places where divine inspiration lives.

The goal is to get a rough draft onto the page so you have something concrete to work with when you're ready to take the ideas to the next level.

Before starting the first round of rewrites, create a list of the changes you'd like to see. To ensure success, give yourself a specific timetable for completion. Strive to fix two to three elements or pages per day.

Frequently Asked Questions

Over the years, my creative writing students have amassed a number of questions about dialogue that I thought would be fun to share. The topics run the gamut from technology to crafting characters of color, so I encourage you to skim through the whole chapter because there is a little something for everyone.

How do I represent a text conversation?

Left and right justify to mimic the layout of the speech bubbles that you see when having an exchange on an iPhone.

You could also format the text conversation like a transcript with the person's name followed by a colon then the words. Start a new paragraph for each response. Follow the pattern of name, colon, conversation.

> JOHN: You up?
>
> MARY: New phone. Who dis?

Regardless, you don't need quotation marks since these aren't words spoken aloud. This is a different medium and how you represent it should indicate that even if all you do thereafter is change the font, which seems to be the emerging industry preference. However, the layout will ultimately be up to your publisher. If you're an indie author, then you can make those decisions based on the capabilities of your formatting software.

Telephone conversations would be handled the same as normal outward spoken dialogue with the simple addition of some indication that they've engaged in a call.

At the end of the day, this is something your editor will assist you with since each publisher has their preference.

What about emojis?

If you're writing a young adult novel where that seems appropriate, then fine. But the truth is that as a writer, you should work to convey emotion through dialogue, action, narration, and characterization.

Ask yourself what the emoji usage is ultimately meant to bring to your story. Is it meant to add to the atmosphere or setting as seen in Gretchen McNeil's #MurderTrending Series? If so, great! As long as you have a legitimate reason for the inclusion, your audience (agent or editor) will approve.

What are some tips for writing children's dialogue?

Word choice is key. Recognize that a child's vocabulary is going to be limited. They may even make up their own words by mashing common ones together to give meaning to concepts they aren't able to properly articulate such as *sammich* or *cattapitter*.

You may also want to think about how focused or unfocused they are on the topic of the conversation. Children often veer from one topic to another as their minds alight on something new. These can be true non-sequiturs or simply something in the exchange that reminds them of something else—for example, an allusion to alligators prompts the child to ask for a glass of Gatorade.

What I find works to help build those swings in a realistic way is to use an improv warmup called Song Circle. In the game, one player starts singing a real song. The player next to her in the circle tries to chime in as quickly as possible using one of the words from the last line sung. The goal is to use the word or its imagery to spark the starting line for the new song. For instance, "Home Sweet Home" leads to "Our

House" which leads to "Jailhouse Rock" which leads to "Rock and Roll All Nite," et cetera. Now, quite obviously, you wouldn't use songs, you'd use things that equate to the inner life of the kid character.

Nevertheless, I find this is a good way to emulate the stream of consciousness in a child's speech because out of context, this seems random. However, if you know the rules of the game, it makes perfect sense. The same could be said with a child's thinking—each statement makes perfect sense to them even if it doesn't for us.

Listen to children's conversations. How do they interact when on one's around? What do they talk about? How do they respond to authority?

In addition, it wouldn't hurt to read some popular middle grade fiction or look for stories written by children in your target age group. Figure out what kids like to read and why. Determine what makes the language in those works different from adult fare. It may also help to research children's behavioral stages. What kind of social skills do kids have for the age you're targeting? How can that be reflected in your dialogue?

Once you've written some material, share that work with a kids' group and solicit their feedback. Do the characters sound believable? To get yourself warmed up, it may help to recall a visceral childhood experience. Utilize sensory language to describe the event from your childhood perspective.

Take writing children's dialogue as seriously as you would anything else. Your exchanges will still need to advance the plot as well as contain conflict and tension.

Lastly, make sure if you're telling portions of the story through the eyes of a child, you have a specific reason for the choice. Perhaps their innocence allows you to place a strong emphasis on your themes of corruption and hate. Or maybe their naiveté lends to the tension because they are overlooking or misinterpreting clues that unravel the overarching mystery.

If you need more suggestions, join a writers' group that focuses on children's stories. Networking with other writers is a great way to become inspired:

- Society for Children's Book Writers and Illustrators – https://www.scbwi.org/
- The Children's Writer's Guild - https://www.childrenswritersguild.com/

How much dialect is too much?

Less is more. Since dialect is often used to denote race and/or ethnicity, we don't want to offend or make it appear as if we are disparaging anyone. So it is always best to simply make some kind of subtle statement early on and sprinkle in just a few words per scene. The audience's imagination will do the rest.

If still in doubt, find a current popular novel that's been praised for doing it right and model that writer's approach. Just remember that "current" in this instance is something published within the last four years. Avoid the classics because thoughts on fiction have changed significantly since the turn of the century.

If I am using a foreign phrase, do I need to translate it?

Not in the conventional sense. That is to say, if you're writing genre fiction, you do not need to put in a footnote or follow the phrase with the translations in parenthesis. Doing this has the potential to break the narrative flow and often doesn't look very clean on the page.

What works best is to make the meaning of the phrase decipherable through the scene's action or the context. For example, the definition can be made clear from the way the person spoken to responds or from the content of the speaker's overall monologue. Consider a film like *Ocean's Eleven* (2001) where Yen (Shaobo Qin) only speaks Mandarin, but all of the other characters understand him perfectly. Their responses, which remain in English, give us a clear understanding of what Yen says without the use of subtitles. A similar device is used with Groot in *Guardians of the Galaxy* (2014), so this approach can work even if you're using a foreign language that's rooted in fantasy.

Another alternative is to add a glossary to your novel if you have an extensive number of words that require translation, but don't fall for the temptation to overexplain in the main text. Trust that your audience is willing to immerse themselves in the culture.

I have characters in my book whose background differs from my own. How do I approach writing dialogue that's both respectful and authentic?

Release yourself from the pressure of perfection when writing your diverse character. Naturally, you're aiming for a realistic depiction, but your status as an outsider makes authenticity impossible. Besides, authenticity implies there's only one way to be Asian or gay or disabled, et cetera. We all know life varies from person to person. Make your goal to create a fully fleshed human being whose emotional complexities drive the story.

But with that said, the brainstorming and research you do for this character can't simply come from your peer circle. You need to do some research to identify and understand what things people in that community or culture find offensive and incorrect with regard to their portrayal in the current social landscape. Avoid committing the same offenses as previous artists and learn to identify stereotypes by seriously considering the problems of other groups without judgment.

Moreover, put aside your assumptions about diversity. Most people learn about other communities through depictions in the media. These are often an exaggeration and therefore not reliable. Read a variety of literature—fiction, non-fiction, historical, and contemporary—written by the people whose culture you plan to represent. Again, the best way to learn how to describe the issues of a community is to uncover and examine the topics most vital to them. This will give you fodder for the character's inner life rather than focusing on their outward appearance. All characterizations, and hence all dialogue, starts from within.

Do I need to use quotation marks?

There are several schools of thought on this question, but the short answer is this:

The act of eliminating basic punctuation like quotation marks is considered experimental and isn't the norm for genre fiction. Therefore, if you want to be traditionally published or you're an indie author targeting the commercial market, you should use quotes. You don't want to tax the audience's patience or goodwill. Make it easy for readers to understand your story, and don't give audiences or editors reason to discount your work or label it as amateurish.

After all, the publishing industry is notorious for gatekeeping, and the tiniest thing, like the lack of quotes, could throw a manuscript out of contention even if it's excellent. Err on the side of caution and do everything you can to produce a professional product because that will increase your chances of success.

Once you have a book contract, you can also discuss this with your publisher. They will probably say that if you'd like to dispense with using quotation marks, you should have a strong plot-related reason for doing so, such as blurring the lines between thought and speech for an imaginary conversation with a dead relative or pet. In other words, your choice shouldn't be about breaking the rules because you don't like them, it should be about maximizing the creativity and accessibility of your art. For example, Genevieve Hudson's debut novel *Boys of Alabama* (2020) focuses on a young man who immigrates to the American South from Germany and has to adapt to a new language and culture. The writing itself reflects that challenge by removing the normal anchors (i.e. quotation marks) the audience would use to acclimate themselves to the text.

And lastly, I'd be remiss if I didn't mention that there are many literary historians who might answer this question by stating that Gertrude Stein, and several artists associated with the Modernist movement, chose to avoid the use of quotation marks. For instance, in "Poetry and Grammar," the final essay in Stein's 1935 *Lectures in America*, she notes that quotation marks along with question marks ". . . are unnecessary, they are ugly, they spoil the line of the writing or the printing . . ."

Similarly, genre writer Cormac McCarthy, best known for *No Country for Old Men* (2005) and *All the Pretty Horses* (1992), doesn't use quotation marks nor semicolons and sometimes eliminates the apostrophe from his contractions and possessive words. He told Oprah Winfrey in an interview for her 2007 book club pick, *The Road* (2006), that ". . . there's no reason to, you know, block the page up with weird little marks. I mean, if you write properly, you shouldn't have to punctuate." Later in the conversation, he shares an anecdote from his college years to illustrate that writers should reduce the amount of punctuation to make things simpler for the reader.

Stein and McCarthy make compelling arguments. However, just because we can sometimes extract dialogue from the narrative doesn't mean that quotation marks are useless. Why run the risk of confusing the reader during the points in the story when action, thought, narrative, and description combine, especially if that problem can be preempted by a simple piece of punctuation?

The open and close quotes help the audience to differentiate between outward expression and inward thought. They are the signposts that allow the reader to discover dialogue and decipher subtext without needing to read and reread passages several times. I'd argue that in our Digital Age, when so many people are skimming rather than close reading, pieces of punctuation that direct attention, like the double quotes, are more essential than ever.

Just remember, at the end of the day, reading is a form of escape for most people, so give them the roadmap they'll need to transition into your world.

How do I use dialogue to convey that a character is drunk or high?

Most people who are under the influence are usually trying very hard to convince the people around them that the opposite is true. Therefore, the best advice for writing such characters is to develop a speech pattern that involves them overexaggerating or overcorrecting their normal speech and observations. At the same time, people who are inebriated are often at their most honest and their most vulnerable, so this may also be a wonderful moment for confessions, confrontations, and the exposure of secrets.

Non-sequiturs are also a great indicator since most drunks have a hard time staying on topic since their minds become curious about many things at once. This will help with creating material that sounds somewhat awkward and off-kilter in a manner that's immediately recognizable to the reader. But while this acts as an excellent indicator of drunkenness, it does present the challenge of ensuring that the scene fulfills its purpose and that this character still has a specific agenda that plays into the scene's conflict. In other words, be conscious of keeping the scene on task.

Avoid outright slurring. If you must do a vocal trick, maybe, choose just one or two specific words that the person has trouble pronouncing while under the influence. This person may also lose their focus or train of thought more than normal, so there's an opportunity to play with pauses, silence, or trailing off via the use a few ellipses. Again, do this sparingly. We don't want the creation of this character to become an annoyance for the reader.

You could also incorporate physicality that shows signs of lost agility, speed, awareness whether that be crashing into things or a misinterpretation of the actions of others. And of course, your character could have lowered inhibitions where they are now willing to do things that they found appalling in earlier scenes.

How do you show something like slow talkers, close talkers, fast talkers, or volume?

Slow talkers are easy. Perhaps these leisurely linguists are people who struggle for the right word, tell rambling stories, or complain of constantly being cut off because they take too long to get to the point. You can have also these characters trail off as if lost in thought as represented by the ellipsis.

Close talkers may be harder to show through dialogue, so use action beats about proximity or narrative reflections that explain how impressed or annoyed the viewpoint character may be about that person's body odor, breath, personality, et cetera.

For fast talkers, describe their pace and cadence when initially introduced, maybe string a few words together for added effect, then only allude to their speed intermittently after that. This is actually the best way to work with speech patterns of all kinds—lisps, stutters, dialects, accents, et cetera. Merely give small indications here and there so the reader doesn't get overwhelmed. We want them to stay focused on the story, not the special effects.

As for volume, simile, metaphor, and onomatopoeia are always great options. *His voice echoed through my head like a rusty buzz saw.*

I'm not a big fan of eavesdropping on people's conversations to learn more about how real people speak. Do you have any other suggestions?

Read 911 transcripts to see how people respond under pressure and how law enforcement professionals handle those interactions. I also recommend obtaining copies of trial transcripts to better understand criminal procedures and the kinds of questions that emerge during direct examination versus cross-examination. You can also use trial transcripts to gain a distinction between the types of argument used in opening versus closing statements.

But what may really help is to meditate on *why* people talk. The main reason is to exchange information. But as you do more research, you'll notice that people use speech to bury their true feelings, to attack and manipulate others, and to defend their position. Use this knowledge to advance your genre's story conventions. For example, if you're a mystery writer use direct and indirect speech to plant clues, provide misdirection, and develop foreshadowing. Romance writers can use dialogue to explore emotion and profess love. Horror writers should use their dialogue to provoke dread. And of course, all writers can use internal monologue and direct speech to demonstrate their characters' morals, values, and loyalties.

What are some tips for writing dialogue for film or television?

As visual mediums, the dialogue doesn't need to be as descriptive and you certainly don't need to worry about dialogue tags, actions beats, or attributing adverbs because the formatting is different. However, conflict, characterization, motivation, and tension are still major elements in developing a strong plot, so I would highly suggest investing in a screenwriting course at your local university. You can also obtain copies of the following guidebooks:

- *Screenplay: The Foundations of Screenwriting* by Syd Field
- *The Screenwriter's Workbook* by Syd Field
- *Save the Cat! The Last Book on Screenwriting You'll Ever Need* by Blake Snyder
- *Save the Cat! Writes for TV: The Last Book on Creating Binge-Worthy Content You'll Ever Need* by Jamie Nash

In the meantime, record your favorite show or film and analyze it scene by scene. How does each exchange reveal the character's personalities and motivations? How does the conflict build? Where does the climax fall? Once you've come up with some answers, write a scene using characters from the show.

Revision and Editing

"The first draft is the child's draft, where you let it all pour out and then let it romp all over the place, knowing that no one is going to see it and that you can shape it later."

~Anne Lamott, author of *Bird by Bird: Some Instructions on Writing and Life* (1995)

Avoid trying to edit yourself as you write. Don't let the finer points of craft keep you stuck on perfectionism to the point where you dither too long over your words. At some point, you will need to turn off your internal editor and move forward.

Follow author Anne Lamott's advice to put aside any fears you may have and commit to creating that "shitty first draft." Once you have all of the ideas out of your head and confined them to the page, you can see the big picture. You have a clearer idea of exactly what the story is about.

Here is where the real fun begins.

Now you get to shape the piece into something noteworthy. Don't rush yourself in this respect, but do keep in mind that you are now revising or re-envisioning for clarity so that the audience can fall in love with your ideas too.

Remember, as writers we have the power to go back and change anything that isn't working. While the initial draft may be written linearly, we don't need to think that way once the full concept is on the page. We can focus on what isn't working about the middle and tweak it until the ending makes sense or vice versa. We have an infinite number of chances to revamp what we want to say until it is exactly right. Nothing is set in stone until you press "published."

With that said, the best way to revise your dialogue and to see if it flows or has rhythm, is to read the work aloud or recruit a set of actors to get a feel of how the work would unfold if performed. Flag anything that feels clunky, wordy, or nonsensical.

When seeking peer feedback, do not send your work to your entire peer group. If everyone responds, you'll overwhelm yourself with information and become frustrated. Moreover, you'll have used everyone in your arsenal and will no longer have a place to solicit further critiques. Instead, show your work to one person at a time. Get their general notes but also ask about specific items that may have given you trouble during the writing process. Revise based on that feedback then send your work out to another person. Work with one partner at a time until you're satisfied, or switch to a professional editor who can take several passes over the work as you make corrections.

Pay special attention to any overlapping critiques you receive because that's a sign that a real problem may exist. Also, keep in mind that if you don't like a note or you're feeling defensive/insecure, you have the power to take the advice or leave it. This mindset alone should empower you throughout revision process.

If you're not already part of a critique group or writer's organization, workshop your writing by going to readings where you can perform your manuscript aloud. Note the audience reactions. Are they laughing, smiling, or giving any sort of verbal response? Are they staring blankly? What's the vibe in the room? Take notes on what works and what doesn't. Do the lines flow with a sense of rhythm, or are you stumbling over your own ideas? Get verbal feedback if there's time. Do everything you can to polish the work and find a sense of direction.

Unsure where to start? Here are some questions you can ask when seeking feedback:

- Is it clear who is speaking at all times?
- Does each character have a distinct voice? Do any of the phrases feel forced or inauthentic to the characters?
- Does the dialogue make sense? In other words, is it clear what's happening in the scene? Is the viewpoint character's motivation clear?
- Can you identify the conflict, what's at stake, and what it will cost if the POV character doesn't get what they want?
- Does the manuscript contain any maid-and-butler dialogue or purple prose? Does the dialogue feel like it is telling rather than showing?
- Is there enough dialogue that the manuscript feels well-paced?

Receiving criticism and feedback is difficult. As a result, your first reaction may be to skip this step or dismiss any advice you may receive about your work. As painful as it may be, you always want to get feedback because an outside eye may be able to bring a new perspective. As the artist, we are often unable to make objective decisions because we're too close to the work. Learning to think through every note is an important part of your growth as a writer. Regardless of how painful or time consuming this effort may be, there's value in the exercise because you may find a gem of an idea and because it will force you to look at your work more constructively.

DIALOGUE: SELF-EDITING CHECKLIST

The questions on this list are extremely specific, so I only recommend tackling this list once you've made several polishes to your manuscript and have decided to prepare it for submission.

- Does the dialogue feel appropriate to the genre?

- Does each exchange serve a purpose like advancing the plot, building character, setting the tone, developing the mood, or clarifying the theme?
- Have I effectively differentiated each character's voice? Does the dialogue feel authentic to each character? Does the dialogue fit their age, outlook, and personality?
- Are all the catchphrases, quirks, and speech affectations used sparingly and in a way that best serves the overall character?
- Does the dialogue create tension and conflict? Are the characters either attacking or defending their position?
- Does the story have a good balance of dialogue, action, thoughts, and narrative?
- Are the characters' goals, motivations, and emotions clear from their dialogue and its subtext?
- Does the dialogue hint at setting?
- Have I varied the sentence structure and used active voice whenever possible?
- Have I cut extraneous dialogue (and dialogue tags)?
- Have I formatted and punctuated the dialogue so that it is clear who is speaking?
- Is the dialogue paced to take advantage of revelations (slow) and actions (fast)?

Exercise: Revision and Editing

Exercise #1: Skim your favorite novels for dialogue. Be sure to select works that were published within the last four years. Study how the author uses the various forms of dialogue to develop character, drive plot, and illustrate relationships.

Exercise #2: Create a list of characters who deliver the majority of the dialogue in your manuscript. Review how you want each to sound. Do they use dialect or have a catchphrase? Are they curt or loquacious? Do they use SAT words or slang? Add tics and traits that will differentiate them and how they deliver speech. Also, think in terms of ethnicity, age, status, and class. Work to give each character compelling word choices and a distinct cadence. If you've already completed a significant amount of revision on your story, consider this examination an opportunity to look for places where you can cut dialogue in lieu of indirect or summary speech (and vice versa).

Concision

"Omit needless words."

~William Strunk *The Elements of Style* (1920), first edition

That's the focus for this section. Examine your text for anything that doesn't belong. Avoid trying to sound like real life where there is a lot of filler and circumlocution to cover the thought process. Stay on point and make sure every word serves a purpose toward the plot or characterization. As with action, writers should endeavor to "cut to the chase."

Trim the fat. For your first revision, study the dialogue. Search for interactions that aren't needed to advance the plot or speeches that run for too long. Ensure the language reveals something about the characters and the action and dialogue follow a logical order. For example:

> Weak: "Thank you, Carl. I had such a lovely evening."
>
> Strong: "Oh, Carl. Tonight was a dream."
>
> Weak: "There's no way I'll go out with you."
>
> Strong: "Us? A couple? Not a chance."

Weak – Before Revisions

"I am so confused." Mike stormed into the bedroom. "Could someone please explain what the hell is going on in here?"

Linda hopped up from the bed where she was sitting with Tanner. "What's going on here? What's going on with you? What are you doing here? I wasn't expecting you to arrive until after lunch."

"Oh, well. I'm here now. Why do you care whether or not it's before or after lunch? You better start giving me an explanation as to why *he's* here."

Strong – After Revisions

Mike stormed into the bedroom. "What the hell is going on?"

"Nothing." Linda hopped up from the bed where she was sitting with Tanner. "We weren't expecting you until after lunch."

"*We?*" Mike glared at Tanner. "Well, I'm here now. Start talking."

Read. Imagine. Perform. Since direct dialogue is based on the spoken word, it may help to read those portions of your text aloud. Mimic how the characters sound in your imagination. Perform the scene if necessary. Aaron Sorkin has gone on record several times stating he often acts out his material in order to hear rhythm of each passage.

If you're not much of a performer, use your software's accessibility tool to read the text for you. Microsoft Word, Adobe Acrobat, and Scrivener are just a few programs that make this easy.

Reading your work aloud will help you . . .

- Determine if a speech or sentence is too long or awkward
- Discover that you're starting every conversation with the same word or phrase
- Identify if a catchphrase or regionalism doesn't work or is being used by too many characters
- Eliminate unwanted bathos, which is a sudden change mood or tone from a serious or important subject to a trite or ludicrous one
- Develop a new perspective of the text and force you to focus on the macro revisions like plot holes and poorly executed plot twists instead of the easily fixed micro issues like the Oxford comma
- Create natural sounding dialogue

If the dialogue sounds clunky, you may need to adjust the punctuation, examine a word choice, or rewrite a sentence. If the dialogue isn't working at all, reexamine the purpose for the scene. Have you defined your everyone's goals and motivations? Are you clear about how the characters would express their desires? Check that each player has a unique voice that they maintain throughout.

Avoid empty parroting. Are your characters repeating each other's phrases? Strike the repetition. Don't let characters repeat prior statements in the form of a question as the beginning of their response. Things only need to be stated once. We don't want repetition for repetition's sake even if that's a reflection of how people talk. Remember, the dialogue is being presented through text, so the audience can always go back if they miss something.

"Where have you been, Parvati?"

"~~Where have I been?~~ None of your business."

"I found your poodle."

"~~You found my poodle?~~ Where?"

If this technique becomes more a matter of one character questioning another due to true distrust, skepticism, or confusion, that's understandable because it speaks to the situation and the relationship between characters. But in general, avoid rhetorical or meaningless repetition.

Avoid dialogue that echoes the action. Don't let characters' dialogue become a recap of the scene's action. If the event unfolded through movement or narrative description, the audience already knows what happened. If the character has something to add, like how it affected them emotionally or physically, then filter the dialogue through that lens and seek to create responses that are character-appropriate but unexpected. Otherwise, if the character has nothing new to add, move forward to the next scene.

Don't state the obvious. If something is clearly implied or can be inferred from the action or environment don't bog it down with unnecessary speech. For example, if you're character is a ghost, he doesn't need to keep making statements about being dead (unless played for some other purpose such as humor). Or if two characters are huddled under a blanket shivering, there's no need to state that it is cold. Allow your text to breathe. This is when you let asymmetrical dialogue and subtext to do some of the work for you.

Conversely, what you can do is have a character say they are going to do something but then have them take the opposite approach or execute a different option. For example, the protagonist may state she is going to advocate for her best friend to receive a promotion, but when she arrives at the boss's office, she divulges information that gets her pal fired. Of course your plot will need to justify this change of tact, but it is much more interest when we deal in contrasts. Moves like this breed tension and audience interest because they must work to understand the character's motives.

Avoid filler words. Do you start each line of dialogue with the character taking a moment to ponder: *oh, ah, hmm, uh, um, er, like, you know*? Instead, use a clear action beat to illustrate that they are thinking, and cut the filler. In real life, people may speak like the first example, but your writing shouldn't sacrifice quality for authenticity.

> Weak: "Er...um, gosh. S-s-s-sorry. Uh, I didn't realize those belonged to you."

> Strong: Her eyes grew wide as she searched for a response. "My—my mistake. I didn't realize those belonged to you."

Here is another strong example of how to show hesitancy or reluctance without using those uninspired interjections. Notice how Glenn simply evades questioning, and sometimes that's enough to show indecisiveness.

> "Who is your employer?"

> Glenn stared at the grimy white wall behind the detective. "Why do you need to know?"

> "You said you were working the night of the murder."

> "Yeah. But...what I meant is...I got this side hustle on Lennox and Fifth."

> "And?"

> "And...that's what I was doing."

"All night."

"Mostly."

"What do you know about the deceased?"

"I don't know." Glenn shifted in his seat. "He's some guy who lives in my building."

Similarly, avoid passages like this:

"T-t-t-t-tell me about y-y-y-your—"

"My date?"

"N-n-n-n...er...ack" Steve shook his head. "Uh...you-ah-still g-g-g-g-going to...um...those night class—"

"Yup. You should enroll too."

"Shhhh...it. N-n-n-n-o"

The repeated lettering makes this a terror to type and read. And yes, I realize that may be the point, if say, you have a character who stutters or has a lisp. However, I'd argue you don't need to go to that extreme to create a convincing portrait. These tactics slow the pacing of your novel to an unbearable crawl and diminish the audience's ability to decipher the meaning and purpose behind the dialogue. Plus, you don't want it to look like you're poking fun at the impairment.

Instead, describe the types of stimuli that cause the disruption. Is it nervousness around girls or public speaking in general? Are certain letters or phrases harder than others? Define specific parameters, and use those as the indicators for a flareup. In other words, there should be a reason for the impairment. Ideally, one an important one that's tied to the plot—think William "Stuttering Bill" Denbrough in *It* (1986) by Stephen King.

With that said, the actual text can display a subtle version of the problem through short blocks of repetition. Trust that the reader will understand and remember the effect you hope to achieve without the exaggeration. Book buyers are smart, and they love when writers treat them as such.

Eliminate chit-chat. Small talk is socially required in daily life, but it's the death of good dialogue. If those salutations and valedictions don't feed the conflict, advance the story, or demonstrate something about your characters, remove them.

Avoid big paragraphs of dialogue. In real life, people speak in snippets and interrupt each constantly. Even when we tell to our peers about a bad day, we often interrupt ourselves in response to our friends' facial expressions or to search for the right words. When you're writing, break up long blocks of speech by having the other characters interrupt or ask for clarification. You can also include the actions and reactions of the listeners (yawning, eye rolling, et cetera) as well as moments of internal reflection to comment about how things are going in the scene. This ensures your story maintains a steady and evokes the sense of realism, which prevents your reader from getting bored.

Another way to effectively dismantle hefty speeches is to start with direct dialogue, sandwich some indirect dialogue or summarized speech in the middle, and conclude with more direct dialogue. This gives the impression of a long statement without putting the reader through the repetitive or irrelevant portions.

Also, think logically about when and why a long speech would take place. For instance, you don't want your protagonist trying to deliver a huge lecture while she's scrambling to escape the clutches of an axe murderer. In that instance, any dialogue exchanged would be short and fast to match the pace of the action.

Pro Tip: Crime novels often include extensive recaps or explanations of motive by the sleuth, especially in the finale. To avoid the monotony of long speeches in these crucial moments, find ways to create breaks within the dialogue by emphasizing external actions such as the sleuth pulling out evidence to support her claim or having her quell physical confrontations among the accused. In addition, you may find it helpful to divide the explanation across several scenes or chapters, revealing parts of the solution in each. Some of the other techniques discussed in this section, such as questions and reactions from other characters, are also clever ways to keep the reader engaged.

Silence is also a powerful option for breaking up lengthy exchanges. Consider this example from *Breath, Eyes, Memory* (1994) by Edwidge Danticat where a mother greets her daughter as the child disembarks from a plane:

> "I cannot believe that I am looking at you," she said. "You are my little girl. You are here."
>
> She pinched my cheeks and patted my head.
>
> "Say something," she urged. "Say something. Just speak to me. Let me hear your voice."
>
> She pressed my face against her and held fast.
>
> "How are you feeling?" she asked. "Did you have a nice plane flight?"
>
> I nodded.
>
> "You must be very tired," she said. "Let us go home."

She grabbed my suitcase with one hand and my arm with the other. Outside it was overcast and cool.

"My goodness." Her scrawny body shivered. "I didn't even bring you something to put over your dress."

Notice the daughter is silent throughout the scene. Since only one character is speaking, the author could have placed all of the mother's dialogue into a single monologue. However, that would have resulted in a dull and slightly sluggish scene. Instead, the author uses silence, action beats, and description to spread out the dialogue, which gives the scene movement and a steady pace. We avoid a static scene where one character is doing one thing—preaching. By having the mother stop to misinterpret her daughter's shyness for tiredness, we get a number of actions through dialogue—greeting, pinching, patting, questioning, grabbing, guiding...and most importantly, judging.

Breaking up the monologue to show the silent responses from the daughter also works to create a much clearer dynamic between the two characters—they are uncomfortable with each other. Both mother and daughter are unsure how to act. Notice how the author doesn't crowd this scene inner dialogue from the viewpoint character. She lets the situation speak for itself so that even though the mother dominates this scene, it is crackling with subtext from both characters.

Eliminate the word "that." We often use the word when we speak, but since it has no significant grammatical purpose, it becomes clutter in written dialogue.

Exercise: Concision

Exercise: Write a scene where you limit each person's response to ten words or less as a way to practice concision. Use the techniques described in this section as well as what you've learned throughout this book. Identify each character's goal. Determine how those desires develop into a conflict. Structure the scene so the tension builds to a climax. Avoid exposition. You are welcome to use action beats or narrative elements between lines, but keep them short as well. By practicing concision, you'll begin to appreciate the economy in language.

Active v. Passive Voice

What are active and passive voice? What role do they play in my dialogue?

Active Voice – The subject performs the action of the sentence. Active grammar encourages reader engagement because the audience is directly involved with the character or subject. In other words, the reader interacts with the scene on the page the same way they would if it was happening in front of them. Active voice allows for easier and more immersive reading.

Passive Voice – The object is performing the action rather than the subject. This approach is distracting and distancing to the reader because the character or subject is no longer the focal point. The order of things are flipped, and it is much harder to imagine how the action unfolds.

> Active = Subject + Verb + Object
>
> Example: Tosh wrote a book.
>
> Passive = Object + Verb + Subject
>
> Example: A book was written by Tosh.

Bottomline: Active voice is often the strongest way to write a sentence because it is clear and concise. We avoid confusion about who's doing the action. Use this approach in your creative writing.

Similarly, avoid using linking verbs (am, is, are, was, were) and past participles (-ing words) together if an active verb will make the sentence more powerful and immediate.

> Weak: The sheets were billowing on the clothes line.

> Strong: The sheets billowed on the clothes line.

Wait! Passive Voice Must Be Useful for Something, Right?

Correct. There are instances when you may want to use passive voice as a deliberate technique in your writing. For example, there may be moments when you need to do the following:

Hide the Sentence's Subject. If you're writing a thriller or murder mystery, you may want to obscure the identity of your victim, villain, or main suspect until the climax or conclusion.

> The suspect was arrested.

Or perhaps, you are describing a concept that you want to feel universal to the reader (e.g. a magical system or history) and therefore don't want to attribute the cause or origin to any particular person, community, or race.

> The fountain was erected upon a hilltop.

This technique may also be helpful if your viewpoint character encounters a situation where they are unable to identify who or what is taking the action.

> I was struck from behind.

Similarly, passive voice may prove acceptable in instances when an antagonist is confronting your viewpoint character, but you want to keep the focus on the protagonist's experience. This becomes extremely useful during extended chases, fights, or any other violent action sequences.

> Harry was manipulated by Lord Voldemort.

Regulate the Pace. Passive voice results in longer sentences, which can slow the speed of your narrative. You may want to deliberately employ this technique to modulate the pace after an emotional high point or extended action sequence.

> Active: Harry rowed his small boat across the lake, but the hidden sea creatures frightened him.

> Active & Passive: Harry rowed his small boat across the lake, but he was frightened by the hidden sea creatures.

Add Variety. Strong dialogue should be varied. We want to avoid repetitive language and overused phrasing. Passive voice can help to vary your sentence structure.

> Active: Angelina Jolie played Maleficent. She grew up wanting to act.

> Passive: Maleficent was played by Angelina Jolie, who grew up wanting to act.

Bottomline: Use passive voice strategically but sparingly.

Recap and Review

Dialogue is the main way characters interact, and the easiest way to show the development of relationships between characters. In terms of pacing, dialogue is easier for the reader to digest than narrative. Good dialogue focus the character's goals, not the writer's intention.

Writers use direct dialogue to create an authentic experience for the reader, to add a personal dynamic to the narrative, and to establish an efficient means for storytelling. After all, it is easier and faster for the audience to gain insight through dialogue than narrative and dialogue offers the opportunity to convey viewpoints that may not otherwise be possible through the narration.

Dialogue becomes easier to write once you have a clearer understanding of what your story is about and what will act as the major overarching conflict as well as the smaller conflicts for each scene. As you begin to write dialogue for each segment of your book, consider the questions in the section that follows.

Once you've determined the answers, it is much easier to unlock what a character will or won't say as well as how they convey their desired message. One character's unwillingness to compromise may reveal a stutter, prompt a story about a violent childhood, expose untrustworthiness, dissolve into shootout, or unveil new information about a common enemy.

In other words, it is much harder to get those dramatic points of contention within your dialogue if you don't have your fundamentals in order. Your dialogue should be focused on your characters' internal and external goals as well as their motives and what they have at stake (i.e. what they are willing to gain or lose). Don't allow them to get sidetracked talking about things that don't matter. That's how bad dialogue manifests. Every exchange must pertain to the goals for the scene or the overall story.

Have the dialogue your characters use reinforce the setting and the actions your characters undertake. Start that language at the top of the scene. Don't wait until the last few moments. This action may not always be a physical confrontation, but it should involve the character implementing their ideas or plans toward their goal whether that's convincing, cajoling, or attacking to create conflict.

What is the objective for the scene? What purpose does the scene serve in driving the plot and developing characters?

What is the goal of each character in the scene? What are the goals of each character? How far are they willing to go to achieve those goals? What's at stake? What are they willing (or not) to sacrifice? How do those goals create a point of conflict for the characters in the scene? The interaction between characters will be heavily influenced by these answers. It is important that you gain clarity here because much of your subtext will stem from characters attempting to hide their motivations or details surrounding their goals.

Have I developed my characters' voices so they are clearly distinguishable? Do all of your characters use distinct sentence structure? Can you edit each person so they have their own verbal idiosyncrasies? Are the character's voices so strong the reader doesn't need tag to distinguish between them? This is something that you may need to review several times while brainstorming, drafting, and revising your scene. It is also the element writers worry about the most since many believe it is the mark of memorable dialogue. Maybe you have a character who stutters and another who has several catchphrases. Keep track of things using a style sheet or create a section in your story bible so that you have a clear way to distinguish those voices as they develop.

How does the subtext shape the dialogue? What are each of the characters keeping to themselves? What do the characters know about the interaction that isn't being expressed? This will influence what they choose to reveal and how the exchange will eventually evolve. Even though some emotions and opinions reman unspoken, they still affect your dialogue and the scene's tension.

What setting will help fuel the conflict or action of the scene? Think outside the box. Work to make the scene visually stimulating so that you have interesting elements to describe as well as potential obstacles (and makeshift weapons!) should you need to choreograph an argument, fight, or chase.

How can I start in medias res? Okay, so you obviously don't need to start in the middle of a conversation. But as previously mentioned, writers should avoid the opening small talk and closing chit-chat that riddles most real-life conversations—that is, unless it serves some larger purpose for the scene or speaks to a very important element of character development. Establish the scene in such a way that the buildup to the climax is relatively short. We don't need to see the whole sequence of events to understand the larger picture.

So if you have a scene where a boss plans to confront an employee about embezzlement, don't start with *Hey, Bob! How's the wife? GOOD. Got a minute? SURE. Could I see you in my office? UM, OKAY.* Instead, open the scene with the two characters already in the office. *Bob, we have a problem with the Anderson account.* That way, both characters have a reason to be on edge and the scene can immediately begin working toward the primary conflict, embezzlement. You also now have an immediate reason to develop more dynamic dialogue for employee Bob because he's going to have to evade, dodge, or deny the accusation that's on the horizon.

What action, description, thoughts, or narrative are needed to further develop the conflict and pace the scene? Even though long strings of dialogue help to propel the narrative, we don't want to go too long without these other elements since description will help us avoid empty room syndrome. You also want your reader to understand how the action is affecting your viewpoint character as well as maintain clarity about what's at stake and how close (or far away) they are to achieving their goals.

What's the best ending for the scene? Earlier we discussed starting the scene from a place of purpose, and our endings should be just as focused. Decide what the scene and its dialogue should accomplish. Once that task is complete, move onto the next scene. That cut off point doesn't need to be the perfect or polite ending. It is always better to conclude on a strong line (such as an agreement or decision) or a strong image (a kiss, slap, or termination) than to drag out the action for the sake of completeness. That desire to keep going is your insecurity as a writer, so cut those extra lines.

What can I do to make the scene more concise? Once you've written the scene, use these questions to cut the fat. Does everything in the scene contribute to the conflict? Have I started close enough to the conflict? Have I cut any repetitive language? Do the action, dialogue, narrative, and thought work to drive the scene? Is all of the information unveiled necessary, or is it better served in another part of the story? Is there a character who rarely speaks and/or has no stake in the situation and therefore could be removed? Are there places where my dialogue tags or action beats could be shortened or removed?

KILLER TAKEAWAY

We definitely want to cut any dialogue that doesn't serve our story—regardless of how funny or clever. However, don't throw that literary gold in the virtual recycling bin. Save the material in a file on your computer along with any dialogue gems you may overhear on the street. You can always use that information to inspire a new character or a new piece. Better yet, start a section on your social media or website called "Evolution of a Story" where you post old scenes or abandoned dialogue. This can be a great way to engage with fans between books and get feedback on your dialogue technique.

Conclusion

"You've got to give yourself room to be bad, because you learn more from being bad than you do from being great."

~Steve Martin, comedian and writer

You'll never find the moments of innovation writers crave if you let your internal editor rule your first draft. So, write freely initially. Don't worry about shaping anything. Trust your subconscious. If it turns out things don't work or it's really bad, no problem. That's what the first few rounds of edits are all about.

Write as much dialogue as you need to get the job done. Go overboard if you'd like. Add all those clever bits that make you feel like Aaron Sorkin, Shonda Rhimes, or Quentin Tarantino.

Once you have a satisfactory draft, read the work aloud. Work to understand the voices of your characters, so you can further hone their diction and rhythm.

As their voices grow, play around with asymmetrical dialogue, subtext, conflict, and tension. These elements help infuse the dialogue with substance and depth as well as ensure some unpredictability for the reader.

When you approach the final stages of your writing journey, you must begin to compress your ideas through the art of concision. Trust the cuts you make will add clarity and focus.

And of then course, rewrite, rewrite, rewrite. Or if you don't have a specific work in progress, practice, practice, practice. This can't be stressed enough.

According to former Florida State University Professor K. Anders Ericsson (1947-2020)—a man internationally recognized as the world's preeminent researcher in the psychological nature of expertise and human performance—the minimum amount of practice required to achieve mastery is two hours and forty-four minutes a day for ten years. You may be vaguely familiar with this data thanks to *Outliers: The Story of Success* (2008) by Malcolm Gladwell wherein he distills the concept by saying it takes 10,000 hours of practice or repetition to gain mastery at something.

Now, although I highly agree with this thought process (and strongly suggest you read Gladwell's book), you don't need to literally start logging hours. But, it couldn't hurt.

Either way, the point is clear: Never stop growing and learning. Put in the work to make yourself better through repeating the process and looking for ways to improve upon it. You're not going to magically get better just thinking about it and where you are today isn't perfection, so keep pushing forward. Use consistent practice to become the best you can be.

At the same time, be aware of when it's time to take the next step in your career. As you learn new skills, strive to hit publishing milestones and further build your confidence. Look for new ways to push yourself by taking on greater challenges, tougher topics, or engaging with artists who are more experienced or successful than you. This is often referred to as punching above your weight. The analogy is one that alludes to boxing. The idea is that if you move up a weight class where people are working harder and doing more daring things, you will inspire yourself to rise to their level and increase your talent in an effort to keep up with the heavier hitters. This will absolutely be painful at first, and that's okay. Remember how this whole conversation started: Give yourself permission to suck because you'll learn more from that experience than trying to be perfect all the time.

At the end of the day, remember to have fun and play with all of these guidelines and ideas because nothing you write is set in stone until it's published.

With that in mind, here's your final exercise. Make a list of your dialogue strengths as well as any weaknesses that affect the pace of your story, the believability of your characters, or the furtherance of the plot. Endeavor to use this book to help you overcome those deficiencies.

Remember, I can only give you guidelines, you must work to refine your own creative process.

Author's Note

Thank you for reading this book. Please spread the word.

Write an online customer review, and gift a copy to a friend.

Join my mailing list to hear more about me and books like this!

Follow me on social media, and recommend this book.

Mailing List:

https://ajthenovelist.com/sign-up/

Instagram:

https://www.instagram.com/ajthenovelist/

Twitter:

https://twitter.com/ajthenovelist

Pinterest:

https://www.pinterest.com/ajthenovelist/

Website:

https://ajthenovelist.com/

Books by Andrea J. Johnson

Victoria Justice Mystery Series:

Poetic Justice

Deceptive Justice

Vigilante Justice

Writer Productivity Series:

How to Craft a Killer Cozy Mystery

Mastering the Art of Suspense

How to Craft Killer Dialogue

www.ingramcontent.com/pod-product-compliance
Lightning Source LLC
Chambersburg PA
CBHW031104080526
44587CB00011B/826